Church Finance
in a Complex
Economy

Creative Leadership Series

Assimilating New Members, Lyle E. Schaller
Beginning a New Pastorate, Robert G. Kemper
The Care and Feeding of Volunteers, Douglas W. Johnson
Creative Stewardship, Richard B. Cunningham
Time Management, Speed B. Leas
Your Church Can Be Healthy, C. Peter Wagner
Leading Churches Through Change, Douglas Alan Walrath
Building an Effective Youth Ministry, Glenn E. Ludwig
Preaching and Worship in the Small Church,
William Willimon and Robert L. Wilson
Church Growth, Donald McGavran and George G. Hunter, III
The Pastor's Wife Today, Donna Sinclair
The Small Town Church, Peter J. Surrey
Strengthening the Adult Sunday School Class, Dick Murray
Church Advertising, Steve Dunkin
Women as Pastors, edited by Lyle E. Schaller
Leadership and Conflict, Speed B. Leas
Church Finance in a Complex Society, Manfred Holck, Jr.

Church Finance in a Complex Economy

Financing the Church: A Changing Strategy in a Changing Economy

Manfred Holck, Jr.

Creative Leadership Series
Lyle E. Schaller, Editor

Abingdon Press / Nashville

CHURCH FINANCE IN A COMPLEX ECONOMY

Library of Congress Cataloging in Publication Data

HOLCK, MANFRED.
    Church finance in a complex economy.
    (Creative leadership series)
    Bibliography: p.
    1. Church finance. I. Title. II. Series.
    BV770.H615   1983   254.8   83-7109

ISBN 0-687-08156-4 (pbk.)

"A Stewardship of Life" on pages 38-41 is adapted by permission from
"Because I Believe," a sermon by Clarence Solberg in *20 Stewardship Sermons,*
copyright Augsburg Publishing House.

"Facts, Trends, and Statistics About Our Congregation," pages 60-62, and
"Checklist for Planning Committee," pages 64-68, are adapted from
stewardship program materials of the Lutheran Church in America, New
York, and are reprinted from *Money and Your Church,* by Manfred Holck, Jr.,
copyright © 1974 by Keats Publishing Co. ($7.95), New Canaan, CT. Used
with permission.

The quotations from Thomas Rieke, page 73, and Ashley Hale, pages 90-91,
are from the September and August 1982 issues of *The Clergy Journal,*
respectively. Chapter 6, pages 100-125, is adapted from the July and August
1982 issues of *The Clergy Journal. The Clergy Journal* is copyrighted by Church
Management, Inc., publisher, Austin, Texas. These materials are used with
permission.

The quotation on pages 93-98 is from Lyle Schaller's newsletter, *The Parish
Paper,* April 1981, published by the Yokefellow Institute, Richmond,
Indiana, copyright 1981 by Lyle Schaller; used with permission.

Scripture quotations are from the Revised Standard Version Common Bible,
copyrighted © 1973 by the Division of Christian Education of the National
Council of Churches of Christ in the U.S.A., and are used by permission.

MANUFACTURED BY THE PARTHENON PRESS AT
NASHVILLE, TENNESSEE, UNITED STATES OF AMERICA

Dedicated to all
those church leaders who
constantly struggle to keep congregational
spending within the bounds of the people's offerings

Foreword

The rules have changed! Whether the conversation is directed to the cost of going to college or the availability of off-street parking or the dress code for churchgoers or the compensation of professional baseball players or the response to divorce or financing the life and ministry of the worshiping congregation this is a different world than it was in 1950.

With two exceptions the church leaders of today who were born in the first half of the twentieth century grew up in a world of stable prices. The first exception was the inflationary wave of 1915 through 1920, when the price level in the United States doubled; but by 1933 the price level was only 27 percent above what it had been eighteen years earlier. The second exception was in the dozen years during World War II and the Korean conflict. In 1953 the price level in America was 83 percent above the 1941 figure. By contrast, the period since 1965 has been the longest inflationary era in American history—and the impact of inflation has been even more severe in Canada. The price level, as measured by the Consumer Price Index, tripled between 1965 and 1983 and is continuing to climb.

Thousands of congregations have evaded or postponed responding to the impact of inflation by "living off their endowment." For a relatively few this has meant diverting the capital from bequests and legacies into balancing the operating budget. For most, however, this process has been more subtle. Today's congregation "inherited" a parcel of paid-for land, a meeting place (in many cases a new building constructed in the 1950–1970 era that required relatively little maintenance until recently) and perhaps a paid-for residence for the pastor. By deferring maintenance on these properties the congregation often has been able to balance the budget. The cost of this has been to pass on to the next generation of members of that congregation a deteriorating and/or functionally obsolete meeting place. Time is running out on that stopgap solution.

In addition, the tax laws have changed and now have a very strong influence on when and how people contribute to charitable and philanthropic causes.

While the offering plate continues to be the principal source of money for the vast majority of congregations, an increasing number are dependent on bequests, special appeals, memorials, and foundations for the funds necessary to carry out their ministry.

This means congregational leaders, both lay and clergy, must revise their thinking about how to finance their parish. This book is a response to that issue. In this book Manfred Holck has identified inflation as the central culprit. He also provides detailed advice on how the federal tax laws can be a positive factor in raising the giving level.

Basically, most congregations have four alternatives in responding to the long-term impact of inflation. One is to cut program and the giving for missions. A second is to economize by controlling costs. The third chapter of this book speaks in a very positive tone to that course of action. The next alternative is to raise the level of giving by the members, and that is the subject of the fourth chapter, on the Every Member Response. Finally, congregations can seek new sources of financial support, and that is the focus of the fifth chapter. Which alternative is your congregation following? Which one do you believe it should follow?

In the final chapter the author offers detailed advice on planning for the compensation of ministers.

This volume complements an earlier book in the Creative Leadership Series (*Creative Stewardship* by Richard B. Cunningham). The two can be used as study books by leaders who feel frustrated by the continuing rise in the price level.

Each volume in the Creative Leadership Series has been designed to offer practical advice to pastors and lay leaders on issues and questions that are commonplace. This volume stands in that tradition.

LYLE E. SCHALLER
Yokefellow Institute
Richmond, Indiana

Contents

At the Start

This book is about your role as a leader in the life of your congregation, especially its financial life. This book is also about inflation, about its impact on church financial resources and the creative responses that congregational leaders can search out for solutions.

Inflation has taken its toll and, during the mid-eighties, continues to do so, even if with less ferocity than in the late seventies and early eighties. But congregations are still faced with a real dilemma, due to inflation, in financing their worthwhile programs, providing staff support, and maintaining buildings, not to mention building new buildings and paying for what they already have. The vitality of many congregations has already been sapped. Inflation has simply drowned some congregations in their own red ink because cost increases have overtaken giving increases in some places. Unfortunately, congregations specialize in spending money on those items that have gone up in price more rapidly than the Consumer Price Index, i.e., salaries, utilities, books, printing, transportation, and so forth.

Take this book, think through some of the ideas suggested here (no simple solutions, of course), and, as a leader, maybe you can develop your congregation's own creative ways of dealing with the perplexing difficulty of managing the congregation's finances effectively in a complex and changing economy.

I

The Culprit—Inflation

Inflation hasn't gone away. Inflation is not likely to go away! Even if those double-digit rates have disappeared for the time being, the Consumer Price Index may remain in the stratosphere in comparison to what is supposed to be a healthy rate of annual increase in the cost of goods and services.

For congregations, that means that the costs for goods and services, the things you buy and pay to have done, like paper plates and electric bills and salaries, are all going to cost more next year. Not very many costs will ever be less than they are now, at least not anytime soon, say the experts.

Look at Table 1. Since the mid-forties the CPI has wandered all over the place. For decades, even centuries, people have had to deal with this phenomenon. Fluctuations during the last four decades, though, have probably been more severe than in any previous similar period of time. For example, the Warren and Pearson Wholesale Price Index (that's not exactly the same thing as the CPI, but closely related), is set for 100 in 1914, but was only 101 back in 1883, at 100 in 1835 and just over 102 in 1793. For 110 years the index ranged between 75 and 193. Compare that to the 7 to 1 range we've had in recent years.

Depression-created deflation (or vice-versa) has been such that the CPI related to 1914 at 100 was at 46 in 1933 and only up to 84 in 1946. Look at the chart, and recent periods of deflation (low or negative CPI rates) are limited to 1949–50 and 1954–56. Keep in mind that the rate of inflation is the percentage change in the CPI from one December to the next, usually. Thus, the CPI number is not particularly significant nor is the year when the 100 is set. It's the percentage change from year to year that is important.

Table 1.1

INFLATION RATES FOR 35 YEARS

1946...........18.17%	1958...............1.76	1970............5.49
1947...............9.01	1959...............1.50	1971............3.36
1948...............2.71	1960...............1.48	1972............3.41
1949............ −1.80	1961................ .67	1973............8.80
1950...............5.79	1962...............1.22	1974...........12.20
1951...............5.87	1963...............1.65	1975............7.01
1952................ .88	1964...............1.19	1976............4.81
1953................ .62	1965...............1.92	1977............6.80
1954.............. −.50	1966...............3.35	1978............9.00
1955................ .37	1967...............3.04	1979...........13.30
1956...............2.86	1968...............4.72	1980...........12.40
1957...............3.02	1969...............6.11	1981............8.90
		1982......3.90 est.
		1983......3.00 est.
		1984......5.00 est.

Well, the good news now is that by mid-1982 the monthly CPI rates of change had at least come down to an annualized rate of about 4 percent, even though no one expects the rate to stay that low for long. Still, that's far better than the double-digit 12 and 13 percent rates of prior years. For the future, 1983 and 1984 rates are not expected to fluctuate much from a 3 to 5 percent norm.

Inflation (rising costs) and deflation (price declines) usually create severe pressures in financing the church's programs.

Yet, our economy has always been changing and complex. It just seems to have taken more drastic swings in shorter time periods during the last few decades than in years past. Government fiscal controls have, fortunately, kept those swings from being more dramatic, but the ups and downs of the CPI won't go away. They will always come and go. And the church, like individuals and businesses, must adapt to that constantly changing scene.

What it all means is that congregational leaders are simply going to have to plan on spending more, probably, in the years ahead just to keep their programs the same as they are right now. Yet, anyone knows that congregational costs don't stay level, not only because of inflation, but also because aggressive congregations change, alter, and improve their programs. As programs change, so do costs. Still, inflation, or at least a constantly changing economy, will remain as a significant factor in the annually increasing congregational budget experience.

That, of course, puts such a tremendous pressure on weaker congregations that they may give up, quit, and go out of business. They simply cannot keep up with the rising costs, even if their program is still the same. The stronger get stronger; the weaker fade away, die, and disappear. Escalating prices, mostly salaries, are often to blame for that disaster.

Certainly not all congregations spend their money in the same way and for the same goods and services. Families spend their money differently, too. Thus, the CPI affects congregations, families, and any spending entity in a different way, depending on how money is spent.

Families that spend a lot on medical costs, for example, probably feel the impact of high costs each year more than those families that are always healthy. The family buying a new home, securing a mortgage, or renting probably feels the impact of inflation much more than the family that has owned its own home for many years. The CPI records the annual increase in the cost of those items, and not all of us

16

spend money on those items every year. Thus, for most of us, the CPI rate is not really a true indication of the increase in costs we personally incur due to inflation. For many of us, the rate of our personal inflation is probably much lower than the often heralded and published CPI rate.

The same is true for congregations. All congregations spend their money in different ways; thus the CPI affects each in a different way. And because congregations do not normally pay out medical costs (although an employer-congregation can do so under a properly written Medical Reimbursement Plan for employees), nor buy homes and incur mortgages (although congregations can borrow money when they purchase a parsonage), nor buy food (although congregations do buy food if meals are served to staff, indigents, at banquets, and so on), the CPI simply does not affect congregations to the same extent as the published rate (although borrowing money for a project will impact significantly on a higher cost for doing business).

Nevertheless, congregations do buy merchandise. In fact, congregations probably specialize in buying those things which have gone up in price faster than the CPI, such as higher salaries each year, utility costs, and transportation costs for the pastor's car. Obviously inflation affects congregations, too, even though the hefty rates of 12, 13% or even 8 percent may not be true indicators of the total annual increase in costs congregations incur.

But what are the causes for inflation, and what are the hopes that inflation will really be brought under control in the near future? Certainly congregations would be able to plan their incomes and their spending more effectively if they could anticipate more accurately the impact that inflation might have on their sources of revenue and spending.

Can Inflation Be Controlled?

Almost all attempts to bring inflation under control and back to the levels of only a decade ago have been frustrated.

In spite of progress during the early 1980s to lessen the rate, there are simply too many unchangeable or unpredictable processes at work influencing inflation to give any anti-inflation program a real chance to work.

Many people agree that inflation is here to stay and that its staying power will be at relatively high rates, perhaps even some day at double-digit rates again. Many economists insist that there is always a built-in rate of inflation of approximately 6 or 7 percent anyway. If that is the case, then coping with inflation becomes even more difficult and more important. Learning to live with inflation becomes crucial for economic survival for yourself as well as for your congregation. The end result may be that all of us will have to change our living habits and concentrate more on efficient spending and increased savings if we want to keep ahead of inflation.

Some economists believe that the greatest impact on high inflation rates will continue to be energy prices (especially oil), government spending, and consumer expectations. Now that OPEC has had control of both spigot and the price of oil for a long time, there is not much that can be done to hold down those prices (although fluctuations will continue), at least not as long as consumers continue their present consumption habits.

In spite of some changes that all of us have made in the way in which we use energy sources, the demand for oil continues. And the OPEC nations will try desperately to control output so that demand maintains the higher prices expected. For, as recent experience demonstrates, when demand drops, the spigot can be turned down so that prices will stay high. By keeping supplies just below demand, a higher price for oil can be maintained. Every 10 percent increase in the price of oil, we are told, raises the Consumer Price Index by 1 percent. And since there is little evidence that the world is willing to use much less oil than it has been using, oil-induced inflation will probably continue.

Elected government officials are often torn between

approving lower spending goals and getting elected. It's easy
to spend the government's money, and too often Congress
will do exactly that because it is an effective way to get
re-elected. Balancing a budget requires hard choices that
elected officials are not often willing to make. But building
one government deficit upon another, with even more
dollars going out than coming into the Treasury, simply
spells more inflation. The value of the dollar drops.

Thus government spending contributes significantly to the
rise in the inflation rate. Unfortunately, though, even those
elected legislators willing to do something to curb government spending can't really do a lot. Transfer payments and
the cost of funding all those programs adopted by previous
legislators cannot be effectively controlled anymore. The
government, almost by default, will continue to spend far
more than it takes in, especially when taxes are reduced. (A
proposed constitutional amendment to balance the budget
could have significant impact on the way in which the
government spends money and on inflation.)

One view for controlling inflation is that increased taxes,
reduced government spending, and higher interest rates will
break the back of inflation. It might. However, that idea has
worked most successfully in reverse in order to stimulate the
economy during recession. Thus governments that want to
stimulate the economy, reduce unemployment, and combat
deflation (recession), for example, reduce taxes, increase
government spending, and lower interest rates.

Another view of economic theory suggests that the Federal
Reserve should keep its hands on the money supply,
controlling how much money is really circulating. To control
that supply, the Federal Reserve has required financial
institutions to put up larger reserves backing their own
deposits. That restricts the amount of money available for
loans made to others. But then interest rates skyrocket. Less
money is borrowed, less money is spent. Recession ensues.

Unemployment goes up, inflation wavers but probably keeps right on going up anyway!

The problem with current economic solutions, say other experts, is that neither of these views considers the expectations of consumers, businessmen, and workers regarding future prices. How do you and I cope with inflation? Is the way you and I deal with inflation really consistent with the way in which the theorists believe inflation can best be controlled? How do we react? Some economists think consumers are not reacting the way they are supposed to react and that that's why inflation continues no matter what the government tries to do. And certainly consumers are a very important element in the rate of inflation.

The view of some economists, therefore, is that when consumers, labor, and business are faced with the prospect of rising prices due to inflation, they will act "rationally" to offset the effect of rising prices. Consumers will, for example, buy durables before the price goes up or before they expect the price to go up. Organized employees will demand cost-of-living escalation clauses before prices get any worse. And businesses will raise their selling prices in anticipation of rising costs also. The combination of all these actions means that the traditional ways of influencing inflation probably don't work as well anymore.

If you and I expect inflation to continue, for example, we will act as though it will continue no matter what the government does. By our very action we fuel inflation by continuing our spending spree. Those traditional remedies for inflation may indeed, when implemented, only make inflation worse because you and I would anticipate the moves and act before they were imposed or had time to work. We have not really trusted the ability of the government to control inflation, so we act accordingly.

Thus, inflation is likely to stay around a lot longer just because rational expectations now only reinforce inflation.

Economic policies that have worked in the past just may no longer be as effective. At least, that is the view of a growing number of economists.

In the face of that dreary prospect, then, what can you and I really do to cope with inflation? How will our congregations survive in the face of such dismal prospects for improvement in the cost of everything? Certainly we will never be able to cope with inflation until we have learned how to recognize and adjust to some of the major concepts that are changing our traditional habits of earning income and spending for goods and services.

Traditional Spending Habits That May Change

In the first place, prolonged inflation produces a vast range of prices in different stores for exactly the same goods. Or different brands of the same product, equally as good as to quality, can vary significantly in price between stores. Most products are sold at prices well below or above averages for the same quality. In other words, you gain by shopping knowledgeably and extensively in these markets that have "substantial price dispersion." You will lose if you don't compare prices.

Effective shopping will save you money in that kind of dispersed market. Ineffective, impulsive shopping will cost you a lot of money. Congregations that continue buying from the same vendors, for example, may be paying far more than they might otherwise pay if they compared prices with other vendors. It does not always pay to buy from church members. A procedure for bidding (shopping around) is as good for the church as it is for any business. It's a way to hold down costs and get the best price for the best merchandise or service.

Next, the old truism that saving is better than borrowing may not be true in high inflation times. Because of current controls imposed on savings account interest rates (passbook

21

accounts), in a high inflation period you really can come out ahead, often, as to the value of your money, by borrowing rather than saving. Building a church building now could be less expensive than waiting until all the money is in hand. But for reasons listed later, the reverse may also be true—you can raise more money to build than you can to pay off the debt.

Anyway, here's why borrowing when inflation rates are higher may be better than saving to buy later. Assume you put one dollar into a savings account and left it there for one year at an inflation rate of 10%, interest rate of 5%.

Table 1.2	TAXPAYERS		CONGREGATIONS	
	No Inflation	Inflation	No Inflation	Inflation
Interest earned	+5.0%	+5.0%	+5.0%	+5.0%
Less income tax	−2.0%	−2.0%	−0−	−0−
Change in value	-0-	−10.0%	-0-	−10.0%
Net real return	+3.0%	−7.0%	+5.0%	−5.0%

Now assume that you borrow one dollar at a 12% rate and pay it back in one year:

Interest cost	−12.0%	−12.0%	−12.0%	−12.0%
Tax deduction	+4.8%	+4.8%	-0-	-0-
Repaid dollar will buy this much less	-0-	+10.0%	-0-	+10.0%
Net real return	−7.25%	+2.8%	−12.0%	−2.0%

In an inflationary time, it appears better to pay to borrow rather than to save! Saving will cost you money; borrowing may gain you value.

Of course, you or your congregation may feel much more secure with savings than with debts. You may not be able to borrow. Perhaps, on your present income, you just can't afford to pay back such a loan plus all the interest, too. Or your rate assumptions could be different from the ones illustrated, thus making borrowing less attractive. But generally, in an inflationary economy, you probably do gain more from borrowing than from saving—as long as the inflation rate stays high.

Finally the real dilemma: should you buy now or later, assuming you are ready, willing, and able to borrow? With inflation it is obvious that next year's purchases will always cost more. So with high inflation (or with any inflation), you gain more value by buying now than by delaying for a year when prices are higher. Here's why:

Assume first that you withdraw savings to make that purchase, or that you don't have any savings. Then, second, assume that you borrow to buy now and pay back in one year the full amount of that loan.

If you use savings to buy:

Table 1.3

	Taxpayers		Congregations	
	No Inflation	Inflation	No Inflation	Inflation
Price savings now over next year	0%	+10.0%	0%	+10.0%
Passed-up savings earnings	−3.0%	+7.0%	−5.0%	+5.0%
Net return	−3.0%	+17.0%	−5.0%	+15.0%

So, instead of losing the net yield on your savings (3% or 5%), you'll actually be 17% and 15% ahead a year from now! You've used your savings to buy now, not later.

If instead you used borrowed money to buy now, the result is even more dramatic:

Table 1.4

Price savings now over next year	0%	+10.0%	0%	+10.0%
Gain/loss on borrowing	−7.2%	+2.8%	−12.0%	−2.0%
Net return	−7.2%	+12.8%	−12.0%	+8.0%

In an inflation era you're ahead of the no-inflation time as a taxpayer by 20% (+12.8% −(−7.2%)) and as a congregation also 20% (+8.0% −(−12%)). You really do gain from borrowing when inflation rates are high!

All of which is no excuse to go out and borrow whatever you can or pull out all your savings in order to buy a new TV or even a new car. It's no excuse for a congregation to willy-nilly borrow to build unneeded building space or purchase unneeded equipment. Every family and every organization, generally, needs some savings for emergencies. And don't forget, you must always have the ability and the capacity to repay those loans, plus the interest costs.

So, faced with a decision in your congregation, or personally, whether to save or borrow and whether to buy now or later, in an inflationary time the answers seem obvious: borrow and buy now—at least from a net return point of view.

For other reasons, however, you may not want to follow this economic advantage. Just don't ignore its implications when you are reviewing your savings/earnings/spending plan or your church program, plant, and equipment needs. Coping with inflation may require the changing of long held habits. You should know that past practices may not be the best anymore. The following chapters suggest some of those newer ways of thinking.

II

The Impact of
the Internal Revenue Code
on Charitable Giving

In a recent issue of *The Clergy Journal* magazine (October 1982), Ashley Hale wrote an entire article on why Americans like to give. The basis of his enthusiasm is in the reports that come out annually reporting how much Americans do give to churches. And it is impressive, for these reports reveal that giving from members remains the largest single source of income for congregations, almost 30 billion dollars in 1982 alone! The future of the church, of course, depends on a continuation of that kind of giving.

Almost every church in the country is supported primarily by what comes into the offering plates on a Sunday morning. And unlike churches supported by taxes in other countries, the only way the American church will survive is through the giving of its members. Consequently, the emphasis put on that simple act of the Sunday morning offering, the incentives created to sustain and enlarge that response, even the gimmicks foisted upon an otherwise unsuspecting congregation to raise more money, all concentrate right there on that Sunday morning action.

And churches have developed all kinds of fund-raising techniques to take advantage of that moment and to capitalize on the expectation of the people to give right then. It is not the purpose of this book to describe or explain those many procedures and programs, but it is important to note the impact that certain techniques, programs, and emphases

25

may have on such giving, especially as inflation takes its annual toll by reducing the net "take-home offering" of all congregations.

Generally there is a wide disparity in the calculation between what the potential giving ability of a congregation may be and what is actually given. That calculation is usually made by estimating total family incomes and figuring contributions will amount to 3 or 5 or 10 percent of that. That is potential. But congregations seldom measure up to that artificial estimate of what they ought to be doing.

People give what they want to give, of course, although many will strive for a more perfect balance between what they keep and what they give. It is reported that in any given congregation, 85 percent of the people may make only token offerings supporting 15 percent of the budget, while 15 percent of the people give generously and support 85 percent of the budget. In healthy congregations one-third of the people give two-thirds of the income.

There are those who say that the Internal Revenue Code may have a greater impact on giving than many of us suspect. Of course, there is no way to measure that kind of impact. Yet, we do know that the Code does provide powerful incentives for people to give by reducing potential income taxes. Many people give because they want to give, Code or no Code. Of course, these people will take advantage of any Code provisions, but their giving is motivated by something other than the law. Yet, other people, and how many no one really knows, do measure their giving by the impact that giving will have on their income tax liability for the year.

The only available statistic that reflects the impact of the Code on giving is that which IRS annually publishes on average contributions for taxpayers in various income brackets. If you want to know how much other taxpayers in your income bracket give, on average, the chart below reveals the statistic for the most recent year. Comparisons with previous years reveal only about a 2 percent increase in giving each year.

Table 2.1

CHARITABLE CONTRIBUTION DEDUCTIONS

Taxable income bracket	Average deduction
$20,000 to $25,000	$ 583
$25,000 to $30,000	654
30,000 to 50,000	883
50,000 to 100,000	1,793

That's not a very encouraging picture, on average. Furthermore, this is only a listing of contributions by those persons who have itemized their deductions. It doesn't even count all those people who give substantially, on the basis of their own income, but who do not have enough total deductions to itemize. Thus, their contributions are not listed in this report.

The impact of the Code on giving, therefore, is probably not measurable, but it is nevertheless a determining factor in giving. The Code actually encourages charitable contributions. And aggressive congregational leaders, concerned about dwindling resources, can capitalize on the Code provisions to encourage greater giving from the membership. An effective program of tax instruction—when to give, how to give, how much to give—could possibly save a taxpayer significant tax dollars and provide additional funds for the congregation.

Charitable Contribution Rules

The Internal Revenue Code rules for deducting charitable contributions have not changed much in the last several years. However, beginning in 1982 a new item was added by the Economic Recovery Tax Act of 1981 that will permit more taxpayers than previously to claim a charitable contribution deduction.

But the rules for those who itemize remain substantially the same as before. A taxpayer may deduct up to 50 percent of adjusted gross income for the year for contributions to most charitable organizations (including churches). Of course the contribution must be for the use of the organization and not for the personal use of the donor or some other specified individual. Gifts to other types of nonprofit organizations, such as private non-operating foundations and fraternal societies, are limited to 20 percent of adjusted gross income. And for taxpayers who want to give appreciated property (that is, other than cash gifts) to their church, there is a 30 percent of adjusted gross income limit on contributions that might have generated capital gain to the donor had the asset been sold rather than donated. (IRS Publication 526 has details on charitable contributions deductions.) For most of us, therefore, giving can go up substantially before we would have to worry about reaching those maximums!

However, the Economic Recovery Tax Act of 1981 added something new to the giving deduction procedures. And the new features may indeed turn out to be the most significant inducement for some people to give more than they have been giving in the past. Beginning in 1982, a taxpayer who does not itemize deductions may deduct 25 percent of annual contributions up to a maximum contribution of $100 annually. (Of course, those taxpayers who itemize deductions can, as in the past, deduct all of their charitable contributions subject to the limits listed above.) Joint and single returns qualify for the same deduction. The limit is reduced by half for those who are married, filing separate returns.

The impact that this new provision will have on charitable giving remains to be seen. I suspect the impact won't be much, yet. But for the tax year of 1984 the limit is increased to 25 percent of $300 in contributions (total deduction of $75). In 1985 the limit is even better, going to 50 percent of all contributions. Finally, in 1986, the rule permits all taxpayers to deduct all of their charitable contributions, whether they itemize deductions or not. (In 1987, under current law, the plan self-destructs and no charitable contribution deduction is permitted unless deductions are itemized.)

Thus, congregations may be able to do something about the threat of inflation to the budget by urging all members, especially the less active, to make at least a $100 contribution to the church each year (that's $2 a week). To do so will give the taxpayer a $25 deduction on the 1982 and 1983 tax return. Total contributions from a lot of small givers could begin to add up.

Tax Planning for Tax Breaks

Generally, whenever tax rates are expected to go down from one year to the next, taxpayers can save tax dollars by advancing their contributions to the earlier year. In other words, a charitable contribution in 1982 was worth more than in 1983 simply because the income tax saved in 1982 was greater than that saved in 1983. The same is true between 1983 and 1984, when tax rates will again be reduced. At least this is true for those who itemize deductions.

Larger givers can generate even far greater tax savings than most of us. Yet, anyone whose itemized deductions each year almost exceed the current $3,400 standard deduction amount on a joint return can save tax dollars by making contributions in advance, as illustrated later. Other taxpayers of course can advance their contributions and reduce their tax liability, too, for the two years. And the saved dollars could be contributed to your church, if you were to suggest the possibility perhaps, thus easing even more the inflation bite for the current year. It can be done in such a way that it doesn't cost your member anything more.

Advance contributions not only help alleviate the deficits of current years, but, in congregations where budget planning and cash flows are watched very carefully, advance contributions can be a plus for the following year, too. Those gifts can be invested when given and then used as expected during the next year. In the meantime interest is earned and yet the contribution is fully used whenever the donor intended.

Here's a schedule that compares the tax savings possible between a gift in 1982 and a gift in 1983 (the same comparison can be made between any two years when the rate drops):

Table 2.2

Taxable income before the contribution	Tax savings on $3,000 gift in 1982	Tax savings on $3,000 gift in 1983
$20,000	$ 660	$ 570
30,000	870	780
40,000	1170	1050

Charitable contributions are deductible only in the year in which they are actually given. A check given this year but cashed by the church next year is still a deduction for this year. A pledge is deductible only when it is paid. A contribution made by bank credit card this year, however, is deductible now even though the bill is not actually paid until next year.

To help ease the impact of inflation even more, you can also urge your members to make contributions of appreciated property. That kind of gift is also worth more to the donor in years of high tax rates (worth more in 1983 than in 1984). Besides, appreciated property always gives a better tax break than a gift of cash. And from the congregation's point of view, such property can either be sold or put to good use at the church. In any event, giving away property that has gone up in value packs a tremendous tax advantage for the donor.

Say, for example, that your church member is in the 50 percent tax bracket (currently the highest rate) and plans to donate $6,000 to your church. More than a year ago that member paid $2,000 for some common stock shares that are now worth $6,000. Of course, your member could simply write a check to your church for $6,000 and cut the family's taxes by $3,000 (50 percent × $6,000), just like that. But the tax-smart move would be to donate the stock, not the cash, to the church.

Your church treasurer doesn't care what is given—cash or stock. He or she might prefer the cash, but, given the stock, will probably go out and sell it promptly and take the cash that way anyway. The form of the gift makes a difference only to your member, really.

Sure, your member gets the same $6,000 charitable contribution deduction (and pays $3,000 less income tax!) as from the cash gift, assuming neither gift exceeds the limits on cash gifts (50 percent of adjusted gross income) or capital gain property (30 percent of adjusted gross income), and of course it wouldn't exceed this limit for someone in the 50 percent tax bracket. But the gift of stock saves yet other taxes.

If the church takes the stock instead of the cash, your member gets a bigger tax break, like $800 more—$4,000 (the profit) × 50 percent (tax bracket) × 40 percent (long-term capital gains rate). That way your member not only gets the charitable contribution deduction the same as cash, but also avoids the capital gains tax on the profit. It's a two-way gain. And with a larger tax savings that way, your member might be inclined to share that significant tax savings with the church further by giving an even greater gift.

Perhaps the member wants to keep that stock after all, yet make a $6,000 contribution anyway. Suggest that the stock be contributed and then repurchased at the current market price. The member's cost for that stock should be about the same as the gift value, and then, whenever it is sold or given away again, the cost basis will be the actual amount paid to repurchase the stock. The tax rules in this area are tricky, so be sure you and your member are on safe ground whenever you make an arrangement. Talk to tax counsel first.

Perhaps the most interesting tax planning technique that contributors can use to help your congregation with its inflation problems, cash flow, and budget problems is that of making two years of contributions in one year. For some taxpayers whose total itemized deductions are just below the standard deduction (zero bracket amount) of $3,400, this tax tactic makes sense for reducing tax liability in both years. Here's the way it works.

Assume that your member has adjusted gross income of $15,000 and files a joint return. Assume also that potential itemized deductions of $3,000 are available each year and that $800 of that is for annual contributions to your church. If your member is financially able to make that $800 contribution in either year, that is, double up in any one year, here is what can be done.

The normal way would be to make an $800 contribution each year. But total itemized deductions of $3,000 do not exceed the current standard deduction of $3,400 on a joint return that way. Thus, the couple gets a $3,400 deduction each year whether it makes any contributions to your church or not. That's simply a $6,800 total "automatic" deduction for the two years.

The smart tax maneuver, however, would be to prepay the $800 church contribution for next year this year (that helps the congregation's inflation problem, cash flow, and budget deficit now, without waiting) and to pay nothing next year, but every other year make a double contribution. The total deduction for the two years becomes $7,200 on the member's tax return instead of just 6,800. Like this: this year itemized deductions are 3,800 (3,000 plus next year's $800 church contribution made this year) and in the following year the standard deduction of $3,400 (since deductions are not enough that year—only $2,200—to itemize).

Encourage your members to do some creative tax avoidance and then give the tax savings to the church! That will help your congregation, make your member feel good, and put more of his or her dollars into the church's program!

Other Giving Incentives from IRS

Life insurance, for example, can be a very worthwhile way for your members to give to your church. There are various ways of doing this, any one of which should be reviewed with an insurance representative first. But, again, it is the Internal Revenue Code which makes such a gift especially attractive.

A person can assign over to the church the entire ownership of a policy on the donor's life. The donor may continue making the premium payments (thus receiving a charitable contribution deduction equal to that payment), or may have nothing more to do with it, letting the church carry the premiums. Upon the donor's death, the face amount of the policy goes to the church.

If a policy is given to your church in that way, the church could immediately withdraw the cash loan value, using those proceeds to help gird its financial program, paying very little interest for the loan. Or the policy could be cashed in and nothing more be available. Perhaps just the dividends are handed over to the church each year. In any event, there are opportunities for using members' life insurance for church purposes, especially so among older members who no longer need the coverages they purchased many years ago.

Deferred giving-while-living plans are also encouraged by the Internal Revenue Code and have an impact on charitable giving to churches. In such plans the Code makes available a charitable contribution deduction for a portion of the gift at the outset and perhaps each year also, even though the donor might receive some kind of lifetime income or even retain use of the property.

A member could give to your church a very large sum, retain a lifetime income from the investment income on that gift, and yet take a considerable charitable contribution deduction. It is a way in which the Code encourages gifts to churches and often has a direct bearing on a member's ability and willingness to make such a gift.

Deferred giving programs tend to increase regular giving of your members rather than impinging on the member's current giving. As the vision of what can be done through greater giving catches on, it spills over into current giving as well as long-term giving.

Some of your members will not want to give while living, so may designate in their wills sums for the church. Here again the Federal estate laws encourage such gifts by allowing charitable contributions as an exclusion from taxable estate. The giving-while-living gift offers the greater advantage sooner, generally, but members can certainly be encouraged to give gifts from their estates as well. The tax laws are helpful in developing an interest in such giving.

Is the Offering Envelope Still Needed?

Many people now receive monthly or semi-monthly paychecks. These same people may receive quarterly or semiannual interest and dividend payments. Non-employee income is part of the earnings pattern of many Americans. Yet we continue to urge our people to give weekly. "The firstfruits" generally means that the first part of our incomes is to go to charitable purposes, but is it consistent with the way in which people actually receive their incomes to encourage "weekly" giving?

Furthermore, people may make an annual gift at year-end after they have estimated what their tax liability is going to be. And it is possible to use a credit card for offerings to the church. Does that mean, then, that the weekly offering envelope is outmoded, a relic of the past that should be discarded for more modern procedures that fit better into the way Americans really earn and give?

I think the weekly offering envelope has a very important part to play in the way we give, in the way we worship, and in the way churches should go about collecting the money they need to operate in the coming decades. Cost-cutting steps that eliminate the weekly envelope from the budget may be only the prelude to financial disaster for a congregation that is fighting the inroads of inflation on its total income anyway. I think the weekly offering envelope can be an important inflation fighter by keeping offerings higher than they would be otherwise.

1. The weekly offering envelope is a convenient vehicle for placing money in an offering plate. Of course, bills and checks can be placed in the offering receptacle just as easily, but for many people, being able to place their money into an envelope and then putting the envelope into the plate is a convenience that encourages their giving habits.

2. The weekly offering envelope box that sits on the bedroom chest of drawers (or wherever it reposes) is a weekly reminder to the church member of his or her intentions to give. Unused envelopes are an embarrassment. Even the irregular churchgoer may use back envelopes for catch-up giving, something that might not be done if the unused envelope were not there as a reminder.

3. Most church offering envelopes carry a brief, pertinent stewardship message on the outside, another reminder of the member's response to God's love and the needs of the church for that offering. Some people don't read the message, of course, but for those who do, it is a frequent reminder of the importance of regular stewardship habits and of giving.

4. Some families still retain the important family financial planning practice of dividing the regular paycheck according to the categories of a family budget. One category for church members will be contributions. A set of weekly offering envelopes provides a convenient place to put that "set-aside" money until it is placed in the offering plate. Offering

35

envelopes can be helpful in the family budget-planning process.

5. Where congregations have several funds needing money, the offering envelopes provide a convenient way for members to give a total sum and then divide it up according to their choice, marking that division on the outside of the envelope. A single-pocket envelope would always seem desirable no matter how many funds are designated. Putting cash or checks into more than one pocket is inefficient and unnecessary and often very inconvenient. But the marking of the purpose for the intended gift on the outside of the envelope is extremely useful for the donor and for the financial secretary.

6. Of course, the weekly offering envelope provides an accurate record of giving that can easily be used to record each member's gift to the church. Most people probably do write checks, and that provides them with a record. Some people use credit cards, and others may use some form of transfer exchange agreement between their bank and the church's bank; but by far the greatest number of churchgoers probably still use cash. The offering envelope provides a record of that gift. (From the point of view of internal accounting control procedures, members should be encouraged to use personal checks.) The offering envelope then is also the evidence that could support a member's giving claim to the IRS.

7. The weekly offering envelope also provides an opportunity to participate in the weekly worship experience that would not be possible without it. The offering is very much a part of the worship services in most churches, especially Protestant congregations. It may have been put into worship as a practical way to collect money from the people to support the church, but in today's emphasis on stewardship and the giving of our money in response to God's love for us, the offering has a real liturgical place in the worship service. It is an expression of our response similar to

the giving of the firstfruits noted in the Old Testament record. We worship not only in fellowship with others, not only with praise and singing and prayer, but also with our giving. It is part of worship. The offering envelope makes the visible expression of that act possible.

8. And even though many of us aren't paid weekly, we do go to church weekly. Why shouldn't we also give weekly at the same time that we worship? Our work and living schedules are all centered around the week and the weekend. The weekly offering envelope is one more expression of that weekly discipline in living.

9. Fund raisers will say that the more opportunities people have to give in a congregation, the more they will give. If that is true, then the more envelopes provided to the membership, the more will be given. Total congregational income might very well drop if the weekly offering envelope were replaced by a monthly envelope or done away with completely.

When the weekly offering becomes an important part of the weekly worship service, then the offering of people can take on more meaning and might generate even more giving. Gretchen Marz, a Lutheran lay person, has suggested that "the more clergy-oriented a service of worship is, the more neglected the offering of the laity. So," she says, "the first rule-of-thumb should be to let the people in on the action."

Have an offering procession, she suggests, where one member of the family brings the family gifts (the offering envelope) to the altar. Sing songs of dedication during the procession. Prepare lay people to offer prayers from their pews. Receive gifts of food, books, clothing, and so forth. Use a different family each week as ushers. Report finances in terms of work accomplished rather than in dollars and cents.

People want to give. Americans like to give, says Ashley Hale. The weekly offering envelope provides the vehicle and perhaps the incentive to make certain that the gift is given. And the more gifts given, the easier for that congregation to withstand the onslaught of the CPI on the congregational budget!

A Stewardship of Life

This is not a book on fund raising, and yet in a sense it is. If inflation and the rising costs of goods and services are not being met with an equal increase in the giving response of our members (or cost-cutting procedures), then we must talk about more giving, about fund raising.

But I am convinced that it is more important to teach stewardship as a way of life to those persons who sit in the pews of our churches, than it is to burden them with the dire financial needs of the church caused by inflation. Congregations that go begging keep on begging, while those which emphasize the importance of giving, the worth of the gift to the donor, the need for the donor to give regardless of the needs of the church, will find their treasuries at least fuller, perhaps even burgeoning eventually.

Certainly the Internal Revenue Code has an impact on the giving patterns of many people, and perhaps those benefits need to be optimized (as previously described) in order to help congregations beat inflation. But I am convinced that when appropriate attitudes toward the stewardship of one's life are taught and encouraged by the church, it won't make any difference what the Code says. People will give anyway.

Simply put, I believe that God has created the world, and because he created it I believe that he is the owner of everything that exists, and that he has made me a caretaker, a manager, a steward over that small portion of creation he has given to me to use.

I must admit that I do not always act as if that is what I believe. My own self-centeredness, my own forgetfulness, indeed my own selfishness, make me forget; and I begin to think that the whole world around me is mine to control as I wish, if I can; to manage God's creatures as though they were my own, if I can manage them; and to treat all the things God has created as though they were mine, if I can make enough money to possess them.

Yet, in my better, God-directed moments, I realize that the house I may have bought is not mine but God's; that the car I drive may be registered in my name, but it is actually his; that even the clothes on my back were provided by him; that the money in the bank is there by the sweat of my effort, to be sure, but that God has blessed me with the abilities to earn it; that even my own chilren are a blessing and a heritage from God. In fact, when you get right down to it, you soon realize, or at least I do, that all I am or have or ever hope to be I owe basically not to myself, my parents, my teachers, my associates, or even to my circumstances, but to my loving heavenly Father.

And because I believe this, I must act as a steward. If I continue to use the earth and those things God has given me, I must do so with the care it deserves because it is not mine. In a very real sense, it has simply been loaned to me to use for a little while. I farm corn or raise cattle, handle stocks and bonds or keep books, I sweep the floor or wait tables or sell groceries, I push a pencil or work a machine—all in the certainty that I am using not my own but the Lord's equipment. My paycheck and bankbook are more than paper and figures. They tell how much of all his silver and gold the Lord has put at my disposal. And so I return a reasonable proportion of it directly to him by giving to his church. As a New Testament caretaker I want to give not only the first and the best, but also the most, 10 percent or more, as God may have prospered me. And only then do I invest the rest in everything from groceries to gasoline, from clothes to cars, from books to bonds, all as an agent, handling that which really is not mine after all, but for which I am very much responsible.

When I read about the resurrection of my Lord on that first Easter Day, I, too, am apt to say with Thomas: "My Lord and my God!" And then believe along with the rest of the disciples that "because he lives, I, too, shall live!"

Of course, I would be the first to admit that I do not always live like a person who has been redeemed and saved. More often than not I use my body as if it were my own, and not God's, to do with as I pleased. I don't always ask him where he wants me to go, or what he wants me to do or how I ought to think or act. To be completely honest, there are times when I don't even think about God.

But the Bible is quite specific in telling me that I am not my own, however much I may want to believe otherwise. Instead it tells me that I was redeemed and that I am to glorify God with my body, I am to live as Christ's steward with the body, mind, and soul he has redeemed. My body is his and I am to use it to praise him, to speak for him, to witness to his saving and keeping grace. That is the life I owe.

When I stop ignoring God and resisting him, I learn that in mercy he has called me through the gospel and his Word, and caused sin and grace to make sense to me. What is more, he continues to call me, he keeps on enlightening me, he constantly causes me to grow in grace and in the knowledge of my Lord and Savior Jesus Christ, and he keeps me from falling so that he will be able to present me without blemish before the presence of his glory with rejoicing. And all this he does for me although I don't deserve any of it.

Furthermore, whatever work God has in store for me he does right here, right here in this temple of the Holy Spirit, here in my body. Wherever I go, there is the Holy Spirit. When I need courage, the Holy Spirit gives it to me. When I am faced with temptation, the Holy Spirit gives me the power to withstand. When I need hope, the Holy Spirit assures me of the God of all hope. When I need peace, the Holy Spirit gives it. In the midst of every trial and temptation, suffering and disappointment, heartache and heartbreak, there is the Holy Spirit with me. He is with me in every moment, in every up or down of life.

If I believe that God works in me like that, I will not be able to keep him all to myself. I will be compelled to tell other people about what he is doing to me. I have a stewardship here that I cannot avoid, for the Holy Spirit kept bottled up inside of me will soon be smothered and dead if I do not venture out to share God's love for me with my neighbor.

And so, you see, I cannot worship God with a Sunday offering that is a mere token of my appreciation. Instead I must give all that I can, for I honestly believe that God has created me and given me the resources I have, and that I am responsible to him for everything I have. And because God has redeemed me, whatever response I make is small response indeed to his gift for me on a cross. Even then, what I may think is too much for me to give is never enough, really, for him. Furthermore, I believe I would be committing a sin if my gift were not a generous one of love and devotion and amount according to my ability, because only as the Holy Spirit calls me into this great fellowship, this Christian church, this communion of saints, am I redeemed and made perfect for my Faher in heaven.

God the Father, Son, and Holy Spirit, the Godhead in One, the blessed Trinity, has given me a far more abundant stewardship than the tiny offering I may give to him on a Sunday morning for the work of his church. For that kind of stewardship goes far beyond my pocketbook. It involves my very being, my life, my all. And this much I give him, all that I am, little enough as it is for his kingdom, because this is what I believe!

At least that is the way I see it.

III

Putting the Clamp on Costs

It is no secret. Inefficiently administered churches often waste resources. The better managed congregations know their financial resources, people resources, and building facilities well. With good records they know exactly the best way to use those resources. Any time, but especially in a time of rising inflation rates, those church administrators who can maximize resources will be able to stretch the church dollars the farthest.

I have often said that a congregation can make more by spending less. The thrust of that comment is that a congregation could actually end up with more money without increasing its income if only it would study its energy use, keep good reporting records, and follow careful purchasing procedures to make certain that it really was buying the right quantity of the right quality at the right price from the right source.

To manage efficiently, for example, one person needs to be designated as business manager/purchasing agent responsible for all purchases, inventory control, record keeping, and energy use. It may be the pastor in very small congregations, or volunteers in larger congregations, or an employed church business administrator in the largest congregations. That person's responsibility would be to be a "steward" of the congregation's resources, making certain that all its resources were maximized and never squandered. That kind of careful control can effectively eliminate inefficiencies, waste, over-spending, excessive costs, and below quality merchandise and service.

Constantly increasing prices force us to look at the ways by which a congregation can hold down its spending. Of course, no matter what the times, careful church leaders will be concerned about the use of resources, but the fact of inflation makes the careful attention to spending more urgent. Certainly within the congregations we serve we should at all times be scrutinizing all of our operating procedures—purchasing, record keeping, energy use, maintenance, staff relations, and others—to be certain that we are getting maximum value from every dollar spent. Congregational leaders remain trustees of those funds that have been contributed, in trust, by other members of the congregation. It is their responsibility to be certain maximum benefit is achieved for all dollars spent.

Here are some specific ways in which congregations can hold down church expenses in a time of rising prices.

1. *Develop a consistent procedure for spending.*

Joe Thompson is a very likable person. He's a pillar of strength at St. Timothy, a member of the board of trustees, a Sunday school teacher. Joe is also a salesman. He sells all kinds of paper products for ABC Paper. Ever since anyone can remember, Joe has always kept the church's inventory of cups and plates and napkins and mimeograph paper and envelopes and stationery in good supply. When the annual reports are ready to mimeograph, the paper is always there. Coffee cups and spoons are never short for Sunday morning coffee, or any other time for that matter. The women and men and youth and every committee always know where the napkins, plates, and cups are for coffee and cookies. Joe keeps the stockroom well supplied. The church pays the bill.

Joe's business relationship to his congregation points up a

43

recurring problem faced by many congregations. From whom and how do we buy? Joe considers it his responsibility to keep the paper supplies on hand. The church trusts him. And after all, shouldn't the church buy from its own members?

Well, that depends. Whenever the church has developed good buying procedures in advance, then those procedures apply to everyone, members and nonmembers alike. Joe's price may actually be very high. Who knows? The basic principle for any consistent spending plan is to buy quality merchandise and to buy it at the best possible price. If Joe, or any other member, wants to sell goods and services to the church, he or she must satisfy the church that these conditions are met. If Joe really wants to sell to his church, then he must quote the best price even if it means giving up part of his commission.

It doesn't make any difference from whom your church buys materials and services, a bidding process should always be followed. Maybe Joe is low man, but some congregations have found that bids can be far apart—as much as 100 percent—on the same item. Surely Joe isn't the only supplier of paper products in the community. Developing good relationships with several suppliers and then inviting their bids will get you the best price.

If several people do your buying, it's a good idea to train all of them in proper buying procedures. Most congregations, however, soon discover that control over spending is best achieved when only one person is responsible for approving expenditures before the church is obligated. That's a good way to make sure good buying practices are followed. Buy from Joe, but be certain it's the right price for the right quality.

2. Buy for price.

In a changing economy there can be a wide variety of prices for exactly the same merchandise. Once upon a time you could buy peanuts or gloves or even a camera and know that the price you paid at Davis Hardware would be the same across town at Ace General Store. Not so anymore. When the inflation rate is gyrating wildly, prices gyrate, too, from store to store. "Come on" ads make the prices for some items ridiculously low. But the name of the marketing game is to entice the customer into the store with a "cheapie" and then get the highest price possible on everything else.

Prices vary. Efficient church management requires just as careful shopping as you do in your own family. The first price may be the best, but then again it may not. Don't be afraid to negotiate. No reason for the church to be taken advantage of just because it's the church. Press for the best price. Use that bidding process. You'll come out best.

3. Check in everything you buy.

Sally Simpson is the church secretary. She's a member of the church, too; always has been. And she trusts everyone, never doubting the honesty of anyone.

Harlon Hanson of Down Paper Products won the bid on paper supplies, but, too late, he realized his arithmetic was wrong and at the prices he'd quoted he'd lose a bundle. Harlon was an aggressive salesman, had no time for any church, and was looking out for Number One—Harlon Hanson. He'd bid on the church business because it looked like a decent order and might be a way to reach Sam Einer at Einer Printing Co., a large user of paper and a member of St. Timothy. But Harlon wasn't prepared to lose money on the church deal. So he shortchanged the order, billed for the full amount, and made sure he was on good terms with Sally Simpson, the church secretary. The church never was the wiser until a new administrator started checking in everything. Harlon's contract was canceled and Sally was humiliated.

4. Buy in quantity, stockpile, store.

Rebecca Aldridge was Sunday school superintendent at St. Timothy. She had been a very popular teacher, the children liked her, and now she'd been elected an elder, in charge of Christian education. All the other elders were men, so the chairman had appointed Becky (as her friends called her) to head up the Sunday school. Unfortunately, Becky wasn't too well organized. Nor could she plan ahead very well. So Sunday school supplies were usually bought on Saturday afternoon at the local five-and-dime as needed for Sunday next—crayons, paste, string, construction paper. Some of her teachers bought supplies by her example, too.

No one paid much attention until the trustees started looking back over the financial reports and discovered that costs for the Sunday school were always over the budget. John Karsky, a vice-president for purchasing on his job, volunteered to see why. What he discovered was appalling to his sense of order, planning, and stewardship. Not much later, therefore, the trustees appointed a part-time business administrator responsible for purchasing. The result was a stockpiled inventory of supplies, bought on bids at quantity discounts for Sunday school supplies. Next time around, actual expenses came up more in line with budget.

Of course, it doesn't make any sense to buy a year's supply of mimeo paper on account of discount rates for fifty reams. The stuff may yellow or fade or certainly deteriorate. After all, it's not high quality paper. That's why it's "mimeo grade," rather than cotton rag. Quantity buying is important, but it must be monitored of course. No point in filling up the storeroom with ten thousand plates just because they're on sale when the church doesn't even have a kitchen of its own!

You might consider a cooperative buying effort with other churches in order to get quantity discounts. Co-ops can be helpful in saving money. Nevertheless, when prices are going up, stockpiling helps to hold down costs.

5. *Buy quality.*

Martha Malary was an active church member in the women's organization. She was married to Arnold Malary, the president of the largest manufacturing plant in town. The Malarys had just moved into a picture-postcard perfect colonial mansion. They had taste and they had money. To their churchgoing credit, they were generous givers also. But Martha was a perfectionist, and price was no object. She'd made the project of redecorating the church parlor her personal consuming interest.

Well, the bequest from old Grandma Benson to "provide a comfortable room for wedding receptions" wasn't all that much. Enough, perhaps, to do a reasonable job on redecorating, but nothing lavish. Unfortunately, Martha never finished the job. In fact, she quit the women's group when the money ran out and her expensive ideas couldn't be carried out because no one else would give the money. She knew quality all right, but she refused to shop around; and when people complained about the cost, she was offended, taking it all personally.

Buy quality. Cheap churches stand out. But pay the right price. Two-thousand-dollar paintings for the youth room may look nice, but a hundred-dollar print may do just as well there. An expensive riding lawnmower may be the top of the line, but a postage-stamp church lawn doesn't need that kind of equipment. Skip the lawnmower altogether and let a volunteer handle the job with personally owned equipment. Crayons that are a dollar cheaper but melt in 90° heat are a bad buy. Cheap chalk that crumbles is worse than no chalk at all. Paper plates that are thin as paper won't hold up with barbeque, beans, and salad buffet. Cheaper? Of course.

Quality? No. It works both ways. Pay enough, but not too much, for good quality merchandise.

6. Buy for service.

Herman Skimpy thought he had a deal—a spanking new last-season snowblower at half price from Hardy Hardware, a locally owned store. The trustees were impressed and they authorized the buy. After all, the church's old blower wasn't always dependable although the current custodian, Elmer Doit, was good with his hands and kept it on the job.

The purchase was made (brand of manufacturer unknown), and at the first snowfall, out came the new blower. Trouble was, Elmer couldn't get it going, even with all his mechanical know-how. A quick thumb through the Yellow Pages (just out last month) showed no Hardy Hardware. A fast trip to the store site (across town) revealed a weathered "Gone out of business" sign on the front door. Since it was an off brand blower, no other store carried parts.

Service is important. Buy for price and quality, but also buy for service. Be certain (as best you can) that the store will be around for a while or that the manufacturer isn't going out of business soon. A little more cost to guarantee service is especially important on machines or for any other merchandise that might not be as you expect. Don't skimp here. When you need service be sure you can get it!

7. Double-check all invoices.

Not every invoice you receive is always accurate, mathematically. Computers work well, but people can just put in the wrong data. Don't pay the bill until you've checked over it. Verify prices, extensions, sales tax exemption, footings and discounts. Don't assume the employee at the other end got it right. Check it all out yourself before you pay.

8. Be energy efficient.

Charlatans run rampant here. Extra caution is needed because many so-called energy-saving devices are only gimmicks and do not accomplish the intended goals. Check with your local heating and air-conditioning person or get some advice from custodian Elmer Doit or ask a retired engineer to offer advice. But be sure you get professional help, too, paid for if necessary, to tell you how to cut your energy costs.

Some cost-cutting devices are obvious. Timers for the heating and air-conditioning of buildings for limited times cut use by turning off the heat automatically at designated times. Thermostat controls in each room (for hot water or steam heat) for individual control of radiators will save a bundle. Even individual room air conditioners may be more efficient than a central system for those rooms you seldom use, such as Sunday school rooms.

9. Zone for heating and air-conditioning

Your church building is probably zoned somehow. Maybe it's only a damper that you manually open and close, or it could be an electric, thermostatically operated system that opens and closes valves and dampers and vents and steam lines automatically. Study your situation and then zone for the most efficient energy use. How the building is zoned will determine how it is used. Of course, you can use the building and then zone to use, but that may not be as efficient. Whenever possible, efficient zoning will determine use. And use in summer may not be the same as use in winter.

One church zoned its educational building differently for heat and for air-conditioning. For air-conditioning, each floor of the three-story building is one zone. For heating, the first floor is one zone, but the second and third floors together are one zone on the north side of the building and another zone on the south side. Room assignments, therefore, are not the same in summer as winter. They vary according to zoning.

10. *Compare utility costs.*

Elmer Doit, the custodian at St. Timothy, thinks it's a lot of nonsense, but the trustees now have him keeping detailed records of utility use. "That's the treasurer's job," says Elmer. "She pays the bills, I don't." But Elmer knows about utility use, the treasurer only pays the bills. So a chart has been set up at St. Timothy giving the location and number of each electric, gas, and water meter, with space provided to list the monthly usage and the dollar amount of each bill for each area metered. A quick glance lets Elmer know any large deviation from the norm right away so he can do something about it to cut utility costs. When trustees go back and compare activity for three or four months after some energy-saving device has been installed, they're often surprised at the money saved. Keeping good records can bring down your costs by red-flagging trouble spots.

11. *Automate.*

Used right, the computer can be a wonderful time-saver while generating vast amounts of additional information. Sally, the church secretary, wasn't quite sure she was going to like that new TV screen with the typewriter keyboard on her desk. At first she thought it would cut her work time in half, and she desperately needed the full-time job to support her children and aged parents. But not more than two months into using the new IBM-PC, Sally was hooked on computers. "Nothing like it. Wonderful, easy, makes typing letters, keeping records, and updating the mailing list simple. Let's me do a lot more!"

Larger churches are finding that computers can save time and cut costs. Obvious areas of use are payrolls in large staffed congregations, automated church financial records and individual contribution records, membership information, mailing lists, and so on. The first step is always a careful study of need. Craig Compton is an aggressive seller of computers for doctors. He thinks the church can't get along without the computer he sells. But beware, the church may neither need nor be able to afford any computer. It certainly doesn't need a computer programmed for doctors!

Nevertheless, countless hours of employee and volunteer time can often be eliminated when a new computer debuts in your church office.

12. Recruit volunteer repair people.

No one really ever knew Grace Goodby very much. She was so wrapped up in her job that her social life was often limited. Besides, she sort of kept to herself anyway, even though the Rev. Hoover could always spot her without fail every Sunday in pew six next to the aisle, left side. But Grace eventually retired from her job. Then one day she came over to the church asking what she could do. There was a moment of embarrassed silence due to the shock of seeing Grace on a weekday at the church willing to do something. But the Rev. Hoover quickly overcame his hesitancy when he pulled out a list of cards from his vest pocket with names of members and asked her to sort these out and make some calls. He'd been intending to call these people to ask them to serve as greeters before the service the next four Sundays, but had just never gotten around to it. Now he took a gamble on Grace, believing she might be able to do the job very well. And she did it well. One thing led to another; and Grace is now volunteer coordinator of volunteers, a rather important position considering she can call up someone to volunteer for almost any job anyone needs doing around the church. She's put together a list of 860 volunteers!

Elmer Doit needed some help getting all the heating and

plumbing pipes coded by color of paint, so Grace got some retired members who liked to paint to come out on a weekday morning to do the job. Saved the church $20 an hour in labor costs and they probably ended up with a better job anyway, faster for sure.

It's expensive to bring in air-conditioning people, painters, and plumbers. Generally, there are members around who can do the job, and they don't have to be retired. Electricians, plumbers, or contractors with their own businesses will often take a day off to get a job done at the church. In one church a retired painter spends half of every day painting. Even if the church paid, that's less expensive than hiring contract painting. In-house maintenance is a money saver.

13. Listen to the experts.

In one church a mechanical contractor who is president of a local firm saved the church thousands of dollars by engineering and supervising the installation of a new heating and air-conditioning system in the church building. Your plant and building committee should include people who are experts in the field and who can give advice, supervise, and direct maintenance work.

Almost every congregation has an insurance specialist in the membership. And insurance on the church building and properties is a good place to use the experts. Establishing an insurance committee to make recommendations and decisions concerning the church insurance program and to set up a bids system for the purchase of insurance (perhaps even bought from a nonmember) is a great way to save the church some money. In the first year that one church bid out its insurance they saved $2,500 over what they had been paying each year. The second time brought even more savings, and today they are paying approximately $3,700 a year less for insurance than when they first asked for bids. And their coverage has even gone up!

Trustee Edgar Anderson was on the insurance committee because he was an accident insurance manager for his company. At his suggestion the church dropped its $1,500-a-year premium accident insurance coverage (not liability) for people injured in activities in the recreation building. Instead Edgar suggested the church set up a special fund to pay hospital bills for people who don't have their own coverage. In six years only four small claims have been paid. Large claims are covered by a continuing liability policy.

14. Avoid most service contracts.

Elmer Doit, the custodian, could fix almost anything mechanical. Sally, the church secretary, who was all thumbs that way, depended on her new memory typewriter to get her work done promptly. When it went on the fritz, she was in a bad way. George Heater, the air-conditioning specialist in the church, knew heating and air-conditioning systems inside and out. Ralph Louder had just gotten a degree in sound engineering and had personally installed the church's new sound system (which worked very well).

Use service contracts wisely. With talents like that in a congregation, you simply do not need to buy every service contract shoved at you by eager sales people or service representatives. Elmer can probably do it on almost anything mechanical. George will send out his own crew to solve the problem. Ralph can fix the amplifier himself, if need be. But Sally needs some help on that expensive typewriter.

Even with all that expertise, sometimes it's just a lot less expensive to pay the service call rather than the contract. For elevators, a call to the repair people to fix a breakdown saves a lot of money over a contract. On the other hand, service contracts on office equipment, boilers, and air conditioning equipment may pay off in less cost for repairs in the long run.

53

15. Junk the mimeograph; get an offset.

One of the largest budget items for many congregations is the cost of printing—bulletins, newsletters, announcements, brochures, forms, you name it. At St. Timothy the trustees heard out Sally's complaint about the aging ABDick. It was almost beyond repair, so the serviceman had said. Al Printer suggested a change in procedure, recommending that the church set up a complete in-house printshop operated by part-time help from students at the college across the street. After due deliberation, research, and contacts, the change was made, with Sally's hearty agreement to boot!

As it turned out, the money borrowed to buy the new equipment was paid off in four years with money previously budgeted for printing. And now, after five years of use, printing costs are no more than they were eight years ago. Printing previously sent out—bulletins, forms, brochures—are now all done in-house.

16. Inspire confidence.

It's important that Sally and Elmer and the Rev. Hoover and anyone else on the staff share an atmosphere of mutual trust. Believe it or not, you can save money that way if everyone is free to check up on what everyone else is doing. Everett Olson, the new part-time business administrator at the church, was looking over Elmer Doit's shoulder one day and asked about the cost estimate Elmer had gotten on some valves the church needed in the steam heat system. Seems Everett thought Elmer's cost estimate was too high, so he told him so. Elmer didn't think so, but agreed to check it out again. Sure enough, the estimate was $2,000 too high because Elmer found another type of valve would work and did not need special ordering. Everyone was pleased. Now Elmer even questions his boss, Everett. Mutual trust creates an atmosphere for saving money.

17. Report regularly; compare budgets to actual costs.

It's kind of difficult to know the status and health of the congregation without adequate reports of spending and income compared to expectations. Managing the church from the vest pocket or taking a seat-of-the-pants attitude leaves everyone guessing. Intelligent planning and budgeting and spending and programming are possible only with the help of adequate records, among other things. It's just bound to be, that when congregational leaders don't know where they are, the church is probably in a serious financial bind.

18. Manage, manage, manage.

Any lay leader or staff employee worth his or her salt knows that the more money the church can save, the more money there'll be for outreach and ministry and mission. And they'll do something about it. Efficient management of the church's resources is the key to maximizing those resources in a changing economy. Inflation may abate, it may escalate; but in the well-managed congregation, resources for doing the church's work will be available. Inefficiently managed churches waste resources. Well managed congregations are good stewards of their people and their resources.

IV

The Every Member
Response, Budgets, and
Borrowed Money

One thing that inflation does to leaders of congregations is make them more desperate for finding alternative ways to raise more cash. But in the rush to find the best way, the annual Every Member Response is too often tried, hurriedly, as a last resort. Poor planning creates a disaster every time, and from then on the EMR is simply not considered acceptable. It is often curtly discarded as out-of-date and inappropriate in modern America.

But the impact of our changing economy upon congregational church financing cannot be ignored. Some method of communicating with the congregation and seeking their support is going to have to be found. The EMR still offers one of the best methods.

But what is EMR? In my terminology it is an Every Member Response program. It is not necessarily a visit into every home, although I believe it should be, most of the time. It is not necessarily cottage meetings or direct-mail campaigns either, although it may be. An EMR is a program that gives each member of the congregation the opportunity to make a personal response—commitment if you please—to the work of the church during the coming year. It is a response to what God has done for us, a response to love, a stewardship response to share what God has entrusted to us. It is commitment. And it may be represented by a pledge card or a secret covenant or a commitment statement to increase giving by a specific percentage or whatever. But it is a commitment, it is a response, and it is an opportunity to share.

Some would insist that the EMR is an obligation to give to the church. Not so. We give in response to God's love for us. It is not something we do for the church. While the congregation is the visible manifestation of God's kingdom here on earth and appears certainly to be the beneficiary of our giving, it is only the trustee for that which we give and its lay leaders only the channels through which dollars are put to work for the kingdom. But I respond as a dedicated Christian; I give in response. The EMR is the program that encourages that response from every one of us.

In part, the purpose of the annual Every Member Response is also to provide the vehicle whereby the congregational leaders can get a reasonable idea of what the membership is going to give during the coming year. Following the response on commitment Sunday, a budget can be developed that outlines the funds required for the various desired programs of the congregation.

EMR programs run the gamut as to procedure, from elaborately run, intensive programs to not much at all. But every one of those programs is intended to bring an awareness to the members of their responsibility as Christians. The better planned programs do that. Certainly the programs are not simply to raise money. They are an educational program, informing people of programs, opportunities, and mission. An EMR provides an opportunity to learn, to share, and to participate in the life of the congregation in a very exciting and meaningful way.

Too often, though, congregational leaders lack the initiative to be creative in developing adequate programs that will stimulate and challenge the membership. Thus, the plan fails and the people become defeated and the disasters created by inflation last year are simply multiplied again this year. Better to stay away from planning an EMR program if

57

the leaders are not aggressive, positive, and each personally committed.

An EMR Plan

No EMR just happens. It must be planned. People need to be recruited, an organizational plan needs to be laid out, responsibilities need to be assigned. If not, you'll have everyone running off in ten different directions without anyone knowing what's really going on. Coordination comes through proper organization (as with any program). And the place to begin that organization is with an overall central committee headed by a dynamic, energetic, competent, generous giver.

In one congregation the pastor huddled with some of the largest givers to come up with the name of the best qualified person. They selected one of the best givers, a young executive with experience in managing other people. Only good givers can ask other people to give. And only experienced managers can put together an effective, well-managed team.

The chairperson then selects the committee. Keep in mind that the stewardship committee is responsible for the EMR; the finance committee plans the budget. One committee seeks the money; the other plans its spending. The givers raise the money; the givers also plan the spending.

The intensive part of any EMR is generally jammed into one six weeks' fall effort. But the more effective year-round stewardship program goes on all the time, even though one intensive effort is still organized annually. Effective EMRs, however, don't start and stop just in the fall. They do go on all year.

One congregation in Texas has developed two EMR programs each year—one in early summer for building funds, the other in fall for current operations and benevolences. For most members in other congregations that might be too much, but it offers a significant emphasis nevertheless and has met with considerable favor, generous response, and approval. In fact, that same congregation actually conducts a third EMR, in pre-Lent, but the emphasis there is on responding to Lenten worship and family devotions rather than making a commmitment of money.

The typical EMR program generally consists of five parts—preparation, programming, education, response, and evaluation. Surely the purpose of the EMR is to seek financial responses from the membership. But the real objective is to educate the members about the program of the church and to get as many people as possible actively involved in these programs. Yet any stewardship program should be developed first to motivate people to a greater awareness of their stewardship responsibilities.

One congregation regularly pulls together forty people to brainstorm the programs of the church and to talk about the individual and corporate stewardship responsibilities of the membership of that congregation. That involves a lot of people and gets them to thinking about the life and work and mission of the church.

According to the reports of the pastor of that congregation, each group comes up with creative ideas for mission and service. Concerns are then discussed in various church committees to which these people belong, in Sunday school classes, and in casual conversation. As specific plans gel, the congregation then may vote and implement and support and take action on its various "joint ideas."

That's why EMR success is not counted only in dollars and cents raised. That may be what you want and what you need, but don't overlook those other important by-products: commitment, devotion, greater involvement, greater understanding. An intensive EMR will involve a lot of people and create important, lasting gains that are more than just dollars.

The First Thing

Preparation sets the tone. What kind of program will the church have? What's the time schedule? What activities are to be done? Will visits be made? What about a pledge card? Who's in charge?

The pastor and EMR chairperson sit down and select members for the five committees for the EMR—key people, important people, good givers. Then promotional materials are ordered, mailings scheduled, speaking assignments recorded, and statistical data sorted out.

Facts and trends about the life of the congregation are gathered. The story of the future is tied to the story of the past. Thus the information must be gathered. How has the congregation responded in the past? What's the makeup of the congregation now? What are the future demographics of the group? And much more.

In one church denomination, the following information data sheet on the life and statistics of congregations has been used for many years.

Facts, Trends, and Statistics About Our Congregation

1. Our congregation has or has not conducted an Every Member Response for its current operating budget in past years.
2. If so, this was last done on _____.
3. How many persons comprised the EMR General Committee?
4. How many workers were enlisted (not volunteered)?
5. If some other method than the EMR was used to secure pledges, what was it?
6. How many members of the congregation pledged the last time?
7. How many members did not make a pledge?

8. What is the membership—baptized and adults only— for the last 3, 5, or 10 years, the last full year, right now?
9. Considering all the individuals in our congregation, the members would fall percentage-wise into the following age brackets: Young (to 32) _____%, Middle-aged (33-55) _____%, Older (56+) _____%.
10. What are the principal occupations represented in the congregation's membership?
11. What percentage of the people pledged? Divide the number who pledged (line 6 above) by the total number of members.
12. What is the weekly giving pattern of the membership, by families (equivalent income units, or EIUs)? List number of gifts in each category, i.e., nothing, $1+, $2+, etc., the percentage of the membership in that category, and the weekly and yearly total gifts.
13. What percentage of the people give nothing of record?
14. Summarize the church budget: current operating expenses, special local benevolence, benevolences for others beyond us, debt retirement—last year, this year.
15. Summarize the church offerings: envelopes, loose, special—last year, this year.
16. Is there a cash deficit? If so, how much? And what steps were taken this year to eliminate the deficit, if any? List the conditions that contributed to the deficit.
17. List amount pledged for current, special benevolences, and building projects this year and last year.
18. How many families (EIU) are available for this year's program?
19. How many offering envelope sets are now in use?
20. List the congregation's indebtedness and annual payment amounts.
21. Calculate the congregation's potential resources from the membership's giving.

a. Compute Equivalent Family Incomes: Families with at least one full income count as one, so do any fully employed single members. Wife only, or husband only, as member counts one-half. Mixed marriage (two denominations) counts as one third. Retired count as one-fourth.

b. Estimate the average income per family in the congregation. (Ask your church leaders to put down on paper their incomes, anonymously, of course. Or during a worship service ask each member to write down his or her income on a blank slip of paper. Add up the lists, divide by the number of slips—that's a close approximation of the average income per family in your congregation.)

c. Calculate total family income by multiplying EIUs times average family income.

d. Divide total family income (item c above) by total offerings received in the most recent full year. That's the percentage of family income now given (probably between 2% and 4%).

22. Where do we want to go financially? 4%, 5%, 10%, etc.?

23. How much more offerings would the congregation receive if every member increased giving by 1% of annual income (1% times item c above)?

24. Answer the question: would this amount provide the resources necessary for a creative and growing parish ministry beyond what we are already doing?

25. How would we use added resources? Is there enough for an expansion of benevolences locally and worldwide?

26. What ratio of our total operating budget should be allocated to benevolences?

When goals are set, they must be shared. Keep the membership informed. Continually improve the planning of the program.

The Second Thing

Having done the study, a congregation then develops a proposal. The statistics help bring the current status into focus, but the program proposal sets the direction for the future, not necessarily in agreement or disagreement with the past.

A program committee is designated. An Ohio congregation selected a cross section of 35 people from its membership of 300. Carefully worded invitations were sent to each person emphasizing the importance of the task and urging him or her to share in the experience. Only three meetings were planned.

The pastor explained the purpose of the committee at the first session: "Here is where the dreams of the congregation go from dreaming to conversation to paper to recommendation. If the congregation responds, then they can be implemented. Tonight and for two more nights you will meet to analyze and scrutinize our current programming, no holds barred, from finances to nursery care, from replacing the roof to repairing the furnace, from changing the choir's location to remodeling the basement for the teen room, from sponsoring a refugee family to developing a jail ministry, from considering a day school to plugging the Sunday school in the immediate neighborhood. Your responsibility is to respond to the question: What is our congregation doing now with its resources and what should it be doing to fulfill its mission? How effective are we in meeting the challenges of the economy and managing our resources?"

Specifically, in session one, the committee evaluated the goals and programs of the congregation. In session two the committee took a close look at the leadership potential of the congregation to see how people were being used and could be used to extend the mission of the church in these changing economic times. And in the final session the committee actually made a calculated guess (that turned out surprisingly

63

accurate) as to the giving potential of the congregation. The committee also formulated a proposal of programs that it expected the congregation could accomplish if the membership responded according to its potential for giving.

Of course, statistics showed what the congregation had done in the past, but that was only history and suggested a trend. The larger question was: What could the congregation be doing if properly challenged? Comparing potential with needs, the program was put together. This is what the membership could do in mission next year if the membership would respond with loving, overflowing commitment. Goals less than potential mean less giving, less program, less mission effort. The three meetings done, the committee matched potential resources and program priorities. It then disbanded.

Here's a checklist for this planning committee: (Mark each response OK, Needs Attention, No Need, or Don't Know.)

Christian Education
1. Does the Sunday school program meet the needs of the congregation and of the community?
2. Is the vacation church school adequate and useful?
3. Is the weekday church school program appropriate?
4. Are teacher-training programs offered and attended?
5. Is an employed director of Christian education needed?
6. Are the audio-visuals and video tape equipment being properly used and supervised?
7. Are teachers given grants for training schools and retreats?
8. Are there adequate library facilities for the membership to use?
9. How many adult counselors are available for youth activities?
10. Are church vocations and church colleges promoted?

11. Does everyone subscribe to the official denominational publication?

Evangelism
1. Is there adequate instruction and orientation for new members?
2. Are new members properly assimilated and retained in the membership?
3. Is someone in charge of an effective public relations program for the church and its many activities?
4. Are parents of the Sunday school pupils contacted and visited?
5. How are new people in the community reached?
6. Are church-produced materials used to tell people about the church?
7. Are members adequately prepared for witnessing in daily life?
8. What about maintaining contacts with youth in college and the armed services?
9. Are potlucks, fellowship nights, and get-togethers common?
10. Is the leadership trained in evangelism and outreach?

Ministry Staffing
1. Is the staff sufficient for present and expected opportunity?
2. Is the pastor relieved of administrative duties?
3. Are all salaries reviewed annually?
4. Is an evaluation and performance review customary?
5. Are office facilities adequate?
6. Is voluntarism emphasized, organized, and properly managed?
7. Is the church newsletter useful?
8. Are programs and outreach ministries regularly evaluated?

Property
1. Are things kept tidy, clean, repaired?
2. What about bulletin boards and signs—current, neat, attractive?
3. Is custodial help sufficient, responsible, and capable?
4. Are the church building and equipment kept in good repair?

Worship, Liturgy, Music
1. How about the present Sunday worship times? O.K.?
2. Is family attendance important and is it stressed?
3. Are ushers friendly, helpful, and courteous?
4. Are the hymnals in good repair?
5. Are the music leaders adequately staffed and trained?
6. Are musical instruments, notably the organ, kept in good repair?
7. Are the members cordial to one another and to strangers?
8. Are dance, art, drama emphasized?
9. Are the Sacraments administered regularly, appropriately, and in good order?

Social Ministry
1. Is the congregation's program of Christian service acceptable?
2. What about service to the handicapped, the emotionally disturbed?
3. Are members trained to visit and aid the sick, shut-ins, aged?
4. Is transportation available when needed for church functions?
5. Is there an adequate refugee resettlement program? Is it effective?

Stewardship (not finance)
1. Is there a year-round stewardship education program?

2. Is stewardship understood to be a total life commitment?
3. Are members responsive to using time and abilities, and is that response recognized?
4. Are the children involved in pledging and in giving?
5. Is proportionate giving emphasized?
6. Is the benevolence budget—giving for others—growing each year as a percentage of the total budget?
7. Are all new members visited and given the opportunity to make a commitment?
8. Is the Every Member Response program planned, implemented, and enthusiastically promoted and supported by the church leadership?

Finance (not stewardship)
1. Does the budget reflect the concerns of the membership?
2. Are the financial affairs of the congregation properly managed?
3. Are all bills paid promptly?
4. Are benevolence monies forwarded each month when received?

A dollars-and-cents program proposal (coming out of the committee's concerns for programs and the congregation's response):

Parish Extension
1. Benevolence everywhere	$16,000	
2. Benevolence selected	2,000	$18,000

Parish Expansion
1. Christian education	$ 2,000
2. Evangelism and social ministry	1,500
3. Advertising and publicity	500

4. Outreach programs	500	
5. Anything else worth doing for others	500	5,000

Parish Ministries

1. Worship	$ 600	
2. Leadership training	200	
3. Staff salaries and benefits	31,000	
4. Administrative supplies & expenses	1,000	
5. Utilities	5,000	
6. Maintenance & repairs	4,000	
7. Insurance	2,000	
8. Contingency	500	
9. Travel costs for staff	3,000	47,300

Parish Development

1. Church property debt reduction	$10,000	
2. Additional Equipment	3,000	
3. Parsonage debt, utilities, repairs	7,000	20,000

Total proposed program		$90,300

Resources available to fund that proposal:		
Income from pledges	$78,000	
Income from other expected offerings	12,300	
Total expected available funds		$ 90,3000

The Third Thing

The statistics are gathered, the dreams are down on paper; now comes the challenging part—educating the congregation. That's committee three. Somebody has to tell the whole congregation what's cooking in this church. Here is a job for the PR people.

One congregation put together a whole series of matching PR materials—envelope, letterhead, calling card, note paper—with common logo and then used that material to blitz the congregation with information, enthusiasm, and persuasive suggestions for enlarged proportionate giving. Here is the place to use visual aids, posters, broadsides, letters, bulletins, speeches, one-on-one conversation, so that everyone—I mean everyone—in the congregation understands and gets involved in the life of the church and member participation is broadened and extended and utilized in every possible way.

Another congregation developed a plan for small-group discussions on pertinent issues facing the local congregation. A group of key leaders was trained to help direct the conversation in meaningful proposals. The entire program of the church was explained at such sessions with opportunity for questioning, fellowship, inspiration.

Some congregations have a big congregational dinner, perhaps even away from the church building, using large charts, movies, multi-media visual projections, recorded sound programs, skits, and speeches. It's all an opportunity to tell the people about the church and what can be done.

How you plan to tell your members about the proposed programs of the church is up to you, of course, but an effective "selling" effort with lots of people involvement will effectively spread the word and help the people know their church is alive, vibrant, and creatively meeting the challenges of the changing economy.

And the Fourth Thing

The facts are gathered, the dreams are on paper, and the people have been told. Now only a response is left. And the best way to get that job done in any EMR program is by making one-on-one visits, talking eyeball-to-eyeball to another person, making your own generous gift first, and then going out to tell someone else what it's like.

Visitor training—don't send the sheep out to the wolves. Plan, train, and motivate the people recruited (not volunteers—by invitation only) to make these crucial visits to everyone. Careful attention to details will make the visits pleasant, meaningful, and fruitful. Let members select the people they will visit. Limit calls to no more than three visits per team. Make appointments. Visit on time. Be courteous, forceful, helpful, and understanding, and then listen. Your witness will make the difference and elicit the best possible response.

On EMR Sunday the visitors go out. On Victory Sunday, a week later, the congregation celebrates. Commitments are made and then kept. No one from the church says please, for the Lord demands our response. Giving is not optional because the gospel is not optional. Christians respond to the love of God with gratitude and thankfulness, generously and joyfully. Whatever the need, whatever the economy, whatever the thrust, the Christian gives. We have no choice. The EMR offers the opportunity and the method and the motivation for that giving.

And Finally—the Fifth Thing

Evaluation. One thing is sure, you probably won't do the EMR exactly the same way ever again. But just to keep your mistakes and your successes fresh in everyone's mind—and for the benefit of whoever tries it the next time—don't just put aside and out of mind the current EMR when the last pledge is finally recorded. Pull a group of participants together and set forth suggestions for the next time around. Evaluate. Comment. Criticize. Praise. But put it down and make a record of current impressions. Sometime again, someone will read all about what you did and plan an even better EMR!

The EMR—When?

OK, but now what about the timing of your EMR? Should it be in the spring, fall, or maybe never? It's an important question to ask. Traditionalists would insist that such a program can be held only in the fall because the church's financial year always begins in January. Pledges must be received prior to that date if the next year's budget is going to be planned on time. And, of course, that has been the most popular time of year for congregations to do their annual visiting and money soliciting, but it need not necessarily be the only time to do the program.

Many congregations now have an EMR in early spring. It is really a much more logical time. Certainly in most congregations the church program kind of winds down during summer and there is often a new birth in September. Fresh programs, new vitality, new enthusiasm are generated then. It's a natural time to begin something that will last for nine months or so. So, why not plan funding on the same cycle? Change the financial calendar, if you want, from July 1 to June 30 and then schedule the EMR in the spring for the next twelve-month program, beginning July 1.

In spring there might be less going on in the life of a congregation, especially once Easter Day has passed, thus providing a good opportunity to involve people. In the fall everything new is starting up, and then the EMR is on top of all that. It could get short shrift then; this would be less likely in the spring. Furthermore, many people's giving begins with a fresh start in the fall, after vacations, when public

71

school starts again. To have commitments in hand prior to fall could be helpful. Think about it. It may convince you that congregational response may be better in spring, more successful, and provide for more realistic program planning from July 1 to June 30 (or June 1 to May 31 or August 1 to July 31—take your pick).

And then there are those who would vote for never! Well, I've already spoken to that, in part. Certainly there are congregations that have developed "Grace Giving" plans where no pledges are made or whatever pledge that is made is kept secret, known only to the giver. For some congregations that could be the way, but "never" is not a very realistic response to the need to challenge and educate and teach about stewardship.

Stewardship demands a response from us. Giving of course is that response, and our commitment is a way of telling God that I do intend, really now, to share what he has given to me. I make the commitment ahead of time, not after the fact. I make my pledge before I know what my circumstances are really going to be instead of after all the calamities and good fortunes have occurred. I trust, I commit. That way I will give more generously too. My response is not to the need of the church. My response is to God. The church's program is developed on the basis of what I and all the other members of this congregation say we will give, not on what the leaders say we must have. We all, together, determine the program based on our commitment—not the other way around.

And that's an important point to get hold of. We do not give to a budget. Inflation may have thrown the church's finances all out of kilter, but not for once is our giving supposed to meet that need. It is supposed to be in response. The need will be satisfied, I assure you, when we all respond to that love.

Much has been written, though, suggesting that people will respond more generously when needs are expressed.

72

Designated gifts are often preferred. Perhaps some people do prefer to give that way and are motivated to do so by pictures of hungry children and displaced refugees. And it is good that people give for those purposes to relieve that suffering.

But that does not nullify the primary principle of stewardship, that we give in response to God's love for us. If our giving satisfies a need—and it always does—then we are grateful for the good that can be done. But to wait for the need to be proved and then to give is not Christian stewardship. It is United Way giving! And just because the congregation is in dire straits due to inflation eating up all the offerings, that is no reason to beg for more money. It is a symptom perhaps of poor stewardship attitudes and understanding.

The solution is not a special appeal for more money. The solution to the desperate needs of many congregations is in an effective year-round stewardship program that challenges the membership to think creatively about the way in which they give and the amount that they give.

When our individual giving tops 10 percent or more of our personal income, we have begun to excel in our stewardship response. When it increases year by year, say by 1% of our annual income, then we are growing in our giving, and our giving has become an expression of our commitment. The witnessing Christian will want the world to know about that commitment. The witnessing Christian will be ready, eager, and prepared to make a response during the annual EMR program, especially when confronted in a visit face-to-face with someone who has already made a generous response.

I like what Thomas Rieke wrote in a recent issue of *The Clergy Journal* magazine about the visiting part of the EMR. It answers well the question of why have an EMR at all, especially why visit in every home. He writes:

A lot of us would do well if we were to look at the ancient art of visitation from a new perspective.
We used to visit people because we knew them. The

73

fellowship of the church can easily become too impersonal. Has it? Then begin to change it by getting people acquainted again. Small groups of individuals or couples can be arranged. They can meet for a meal once a month. Friendships will grow and people will get to know each other again. Midweek suppers serve a similar purpose. Pictorial directories will help.

We used to visit people because we had something to share. We still do have that something—let's begin to talk about it again. For the Christian person, faith in Jesus Christ and all the implications of that form the basis of our sharing. We are members of the family of God but we need to be reminded of that relationship. As brothers and sisters we have a lot in common, a lot to share. That is worth learning all over again.

We used to visit people because we cared about them. The times are too impersonal, some say. And where better than the church to change that trend? Visiting can begin again over a meal or to share a word of caring or to give the gift of food. Listening and thanking and remembering special moments (a pastor I know visits everyone on their birthday) are still good reasons to be together.

Please don't repeat that tired line—we are going out to get the commitment cards—again this year. That is more of a collection than a visit. Instead, let this be a time for beginning again the Christian art of sharing and caring, formed into the human ritual of a visit. It could be precious and priceless. It could change the course of someone's life. And it might change the major direction of your church!

A Theology of Giving

You cannot even talk about giving money to the church unless you understand the thrust of Scripture and unless you recognize the response God expects from you in faith. Of course, the primary focus of the Bible is not on money; yet Jesus certainly spoke about money often. Rather, the focus of the Bible is on the self-giving and redemptive activity of a gracious God and on our response to that action. Thus, what God has done through his righteous and loving revelation requires our response.

Now, what we know about God we know through his creation and because of that redemption from sin through the death and resurrection of his Son. In response we have gathered in worship each Sunday (and sometimes in between) because the Holy Spirit through Word and sacraments calls, gathers, and enlightens you and me (as Luther reminds us) in Christian community through our own congregations and worshiping fellowship.

The Christian's concern, therefore, is to celebrate this life and all of this action by God, and then to make a response to that celebration. And the word we use to describe this response to the loving activity of God is "stewardship." For we are managers, responsible and accountable to God for these gifts. Christian giving is the natural and expected response of Christians to the gospel message.

Can you imagine any other response? When you read through the New Testament, or at least when I do, you soon discover that there are no other options to faith. We respond—that is the clear message of all that Jesus taught. He gave. And so we give because in faith we know there is no alternative to Jesus Christ. He is not optional.

Here is what Paul wrote to the Corinthians about the response of those Christians in Macedonia: "For they gave according to their means, as I can testify, and beyond their means, of their own free will. . . . But first they gave themselves to the Lord and to us by the will of God" (II Cor. 8:3, 5 RSV). Our response, therefore, is a commitment of faith, not of sight; a commitment of risk, not of reward. For centuries Christians have experienced the abundance and grace of God, and in response they have given in joyful abandon, even giving their lives.

Don't you see? Commitment is at the center of our faith. Call it your pledge or your promise or your intention, whatever: commitment in giving is the external evidence of internal priorities. What we give shows what we believe. Recall the Old Testament sacrificial system in which the first,

75

the best was always given to God. God was primary, and everything else reflected that prior claim. Those people gave God the best sheep or best calf or best ox not because God needed those things; their extraordinary gifts were a statement of their faith and their gratitude. The emphasis was on the need of the giver to give. Those Hebrews did not give to a need or to a building or to pay salaries; they gave because giving was an expression of their commitment, their response to God's love.

It is clear that the commitment which each one of us will make in our own congregation's Every Member Response still falls far short of what we know we ought to do. Surely we have not really sacrificed very much. Of course, circumstances vary, income and possessions are different, demands upon our time and resources change. Some of us have only retirement income from Social Security, others have substantial investment incomes, many of our members have larger income from executive positions, while some people are struggling to make ends meet on an hourly wage. Some people have no jobs. But because of our biblical understanding of grace, everyone of us is expected to respond as we affirm our need to risk in faith, trusting and expecting God's continued grace and providence.

But we cannot speak of Christian giving without acknowledging that our response will be largely in the form of money. Money, of course, functions in many ways. It is neither moral nor immoral. It is only meant to be used. Only when it becomes an obsession is it abused. Money is a valuable tool to achieve worthwhile objectives. It is a medium of exchange, but it is also an extension of ourselves.

We invest a lot of hours of time at our jobs using our skills. In return we are paid money. Thus, the money we have for services rendered is simply an extension of ourselves. It represents part of life. How we use it, then, becomes a rather clear indication of the priorities we hold and value. If the greatest gift we have to offer God is our lives, then symbolically money is one of the clearest indications of that commitment. When we give our money, we literally reinvest our lives a second time.

But it is not always only money that we give, of course. For we also give when we seek justice, love our neighbor, and work for the common good. Yet our money is still the most obvious expression of who we are, and it becomes an extension of ourselves when we pay taxes or give to charities or support political candidates or give to the church.

But even more than that, we also give by the way in which we live and consume energy and food and deal with pollution. We give our money, too, because we know that ultimately our security is not in these possessions and profits, but in him who died and rose for us.

So our giving doesn't stop with the offering plate. Some of that money goes beyond our local congregations. For the church is a larger community of faith than what gathers in the pews at any one location on a Sunday morning. The church is all the people and is often represented by the institutionalized church denominations and groups of Christian organizations. Not that these necessary institutions of the church exist for the sake of existing, but they are there, like our own congregation, fulfilling our responsibility to love and to serve and to be stewards to others. Money from us to them for others is literally extending ourselves into every part of the world.

And so we give, we cannot but give—

1) gratefully, for what God has done for us,
2) faithfully, trusting God above all,
3) regularly, as an act of self-discipline,
4) proportionately, a percentage, as we are able,
5) responsibly, supporting the work of the church,
6) joyfully, as our joy in Christ may be complete,
7) expectantly, waiting upon God with keen anticipation both now and for the future.

We have no choice. Our response to the gospel demands the gift of ourselves so that this proclamation and love might be extended to the whole world. Indeed, that is what we are about, that's what we do, that is our faith. There on a cross is God's love for you. Where is your response? Is it 8 percent or 10 percent or 12 percent, or is it still only at 2 or 3 percent of your income?

Stewardship is commitment to risk in faith, service to others, responsible use of our money and ourselves, giving in response, not because of need, but because we need to give. You decide what you give, of course. You respond. Your commitment is the external evidence of your internal priorities. And only God will judge your response. No one else will know or care.

Commitment, response, the pledge is the Christian's natural reaction to recognizing God's redemptive gift. There is no substitute, no option, no alternative. We are expected to give, and we are expected to do so gratefully, faithfully, regularly, proportionately, responsibly, joyfully, expectantly. We are stewards, born anew to service. Our gift dare not be only a token commitment, nor simply a one-time matter. Our gift is ourselves, our lives, our us forever. God gave his love. In response we give the best and the most that we can, generously, of time, of abilities, and of money, not to a budget, not to our church, but to God for word and witness and peace and justice.

The Budget and the CPI

Of course it is on the church budget where the CPI has registered the most significant impact for a congregation's financial well-being. That's where the annual increases in the cost of things are felt and seen most directly. And the typical budget preparation procedure thrives on the CPI. You know how that works: the committee looks at last year's figures and adds an "inflation factor" to generate this year's proposal.

It's all quite typical. The final impact on the church is that the same programs are maintained but they cost more. Income falls behind even if it does increase, and the red ink piles up even more.

Inflation has always given budget makers a hard time. Church budgets are no exception. But creative budget making does not let inflation rule the process. It is a factor to consider, of course, but it is only one of many cost considerations that must go into the calculations. Maintaining programs just for the sake of maintainng them, plus the cost of inflation, is not very intelligent program building.

Creative lay leaders, therefore, often develop program budgets rather than line-item budgets to describe the program of the church. Costs are assigned to programs on the basis of current estimated costs, time of staff, supplies, and so forth. Simply adding an inflation factor is rather uncreative and often self-defeating and very depressing!

Some congregational leaders still don't think they need a budget. They can operate just fine, they say, from the back side of a used #10 business envelope. But one thing inflation has done to congregational programs planned that way, if nothing else, has been to catch the leaders unawares with insufficient funds to carry out the projects they had developed months before. Costs went up and no one really expected it.

So, recognizing their inability to cope with constantly changing prices like that, more lay leaders have become aware of one of the important reasons for a budget—to plan spending and to set priorities so that spending can be controlled. Runaway inflation can mean runaway spending if careful planning has not gone into the budget-making process.

Two questions are raised: Why does your congregation need a budget? And how do lay leaders go about generating a creative budget in the face of constantly rising prices?

The Annual Budget Is . . .

The annual budget is an accepted part of the planning cycle of most congregations. It is recognized as important because when properly used it helps sharpen goals and mission, define direction, emphasize programs, guide spending within approved limits, and generally offer a vehicle for better resource allocation and stewardship.

Building a budget is not the be-all and end-all of congregational financial planning or record keeping. A budget is no better than the use made of it by congregational leaders. Used effectively, however, it can be an important management tool for fulfilling the mission of a congregation.

Preparing a budget forces people to consider future goals and to plan for attaining them. It compels advance program planning and decision making. Preparing a budget can uncover congregational weaknesses and expand congregational strengths. It is a conscious effort by church members toward attaining congregational objectives in mission—without getting lost in the details of day-to-day operational procedures. In preparing the budget, congregational leaders have an opportunity to anticipate what may come to pass rather than be surprised when it happens!

Effective budgeting procedures allow more people to become involved in planning the congregation's programs. It follows that when more people are involved, more people are knowledgeable about what the church is doing, and thus more people will be interested in what is going on. Budgeting procedures that involve people will improve cooperation and understanding between those persons and enhance coordination of efforts.

The presence of a budget, when used effectively, will call for an evaluation of each program, an accounting of financial resources used, and a review of objectives attained. Accountability is, therefore, a very real advantage of a church budget. Effective resource conservation and responsible allocation come about when a budget is used to monitor spending.

Furthermore, budgeting can be helpful for instilling confidence in the leadership of the congregation. Accurate, clear, and understandable reports are indicative of careful planning and conscientious attention to detail. Nothing will undermine member confidence more quickly than questions that go unanswered, reports that are difficult to understand, and inconsistent reports on money received and spent. A budget is a clear, specific, declarative document about how money is to be spent and which programs are to receive support.

The budget is a plan for spending. That means it is a control or guide for spending, too. Spending possibilities, however, are dependent on resource availability. A budget helps the congregation attain its objectives by allocating available resources to the mission of the church.

A history of careful budget preparation is an indication that good money management techniques are in fact being used by that congregation. If the congregation needs to borrow money, for example, an impeccable budget history will be an asset. A carefully developed budget suggests the same care in developing other financial statements and in managing the affairs of the congregation. Bankers are impressed by careful money management practices.

Remember that: (1) A budget is an estimate, a plan, a projection. It is only as useful as the judgments that went into its preparation. (2) A budget, like a balance sheet, is accurate only on the day it was put together. To be effective it must be flexible, changeable, adaptable. (3) Approving a budget doesn't automatically put it into practice. Unless it is appropriately implemented, it can't work. (4) A budget is a tool. It does not replace careful management. To be effective, it must be used as a part of the total management system.

81

Varieties of Budgets

There are a variety of budgets and financial planning approaches that your congregational leaders can use to develop the actual church budget: program budgets, line-item budgets, zero-based budgets, unified budgets, capital budgets, debt-retirement budgets, and perhaps others.

The budget most frequently used in congregations is the line-item budget. That's a budget that lists on line after line the dollars to be spent on salaries, utilities, benevolences, evangelism, Sunday church school, insurance, mortgage payments, nursery care, repairs, and so on. Each line item is carefully defined, costs estimated, and amounts budgeted.

A program budget, on the other hand, offers more opportunity for creative planning and spending. Such budgets are organized to reflect the costs of programs rather than the costs of specific items of expense. All costs required for a particular program, such as evangelism are identified with that program. As with a cost-accounting system, the program budget attempts to identify every possible cost of the specific programs proposed.

* Table 4.1

THE LINE ITEM BUDGET
AND PROGRAM BUDGET COMPARED

The Line Item Budget
  How We Expect to Spend Our Money

  For Others:
Worldwide	$1,500	
Nationally	4,000	
Here at home	500	$6,000

For staff:
Pastor's salary	$13,000	
Retirement benefits	1,050	
Social Security allowance	1,300	
Housing allowance	3,000	18,350

For Committees:
Christian education	$150	
Worship and music	50	
Stewardship	50	
Outreach	50	
Youth	50	350

For Administration:
Travel and auto—Pastor	$2700	
Mortgage payments—Church	1,200	
Utilities & insurance	1,500	
Repairs and maintenance	1,000	
Postage & supplies	600	
Secretary, part-time	1,200	8,200

Total Budget and Spending Plan		$32,900

The Program Budget
A Program for Mission and Ministry

A Mission to Our World:
Worldwide	$1,500	
Nationally	4,000	
Here at home	500	$6,000

A Mission to Our Community:
Outreach (evangelism, visitation, etc.)	$3,277	
Interchurch (conference of churches, etc.)	701	
Social concerns (refugees, counseling, etc.)	2,624	6,602

A Mission to Our Congregation:

Worship and music	$5,874	
Christian education	6,074	
Pastoral care (member visitation, sick calls, etc.)	4,550	
Building maintenance	2,600	
Mortgage payments—Church	1,200	20,298

Our Total Program $32,900

Computation of cost allocations for Program Budget—

1. Pastor's compensation and expense reimbursements

Salary	$13,000
Retirement benefits	1,050
Social Security allowance	1,300
Housing allowance	3,000
Automobile allowance	2,700
	$21,050

2. Allocation of pastor's time

Sermon preparation	25%	$5,263
Congregational meetings, committees, preparation	25%	5,263
Visitation and counseling	20%	4,210
Evangelism visitation	15%	3,157
Counseling nonmembers	5%	1,052
Outside meetings	10%	2,105
	100%	$21,050

84

3. Worship and Music

Pastor's sermon preparation		$5,264
Music supplies		50
Secretary's time	30%	360
Office supplies		200
		$5,874

4. Christian Education

Pastor's preparation and meetings		$5,263
Church schools		150
Secretary's time	30%	360
Office supplies		200
Youth programs and events		50
Stewardship materials		50
		46,073

5. Pastoral Care

Pastor's visiting and counseling members		$4,210
Office supplies		100
Secretary's time	20%	240
		$4,550

6. Building Maintenance

Utilities and insurance	1,500
Repairs and maintenance	1,000
Service and supplies	100
	$2,600

7. Outreach (Evangelism)

Pastor's time	$3,157
Secretary's time	120
	$3,277

8. Interchurch work
   Pastor's time $ 701

9. Social Concerns
   Pastor's time for counseling nonmembers $1,052
   Pastor's time at meetings   1,402
   Outreach programs for refugees, etc.   50
   Secretary's time   10%   120
                                                           $2,624

When using a program budget format, the cost of a specific program can be measured to determine its effectiveness by asking what has been accomplished compared to what was planned. The pastor's salary, for example, in such a budget, is divided proportionately among those programs in which pastoral leadership is involved. The cost of office supplies is allocated to those programs requiring such supplies. The cost of all programs can be determined easily using this management technique.

Program budgets begin by establishing a need and by setting goals. Then programs are described which will fulfill those needs and achieve those goals. The form of the budget becomes important as a tool for planning and decision making, for evaluation and for communication. While costs are still clearly detailed for all expenditures, the focus is on fulfilling the life and mission of the congregation in programs.

In the typical line-item budget all costs are associated with some kind of specific expense. Thus, the pastor's compensation is listed as a total to be paid. Office supplies are listed as a total. Each item represents the estimated costs for that particular item or service.

The program budget allocates those same costs to various programs. Thus, the pastor's time spent on various programs is estimated first and then the total compensation costs allocated accordingly. Program costs are determined by allocating appropriate costs to each program. The total for each program is then summarized on the budget. Incurred costs are allocated on the same basis so that proper comparisons can be made eventually between expected costs or programs and actual costs.

These are only two of a variety of possible church budgets. Other budget types include the following.

A unified operating budget provides the most efficient control and management of the financial resources of the congregation, but it's not a particularly popular kind of budget instrument. In this type of budget all the organizations in the congregation combine their funds into one checking account, but retain their autonomy with separate and distinct funds. Each organization maintains a treasurer, who authorizes the church treasurer to write the necessary checks against their account. With one document the entire financial operating activity of the congregation is planned and reviewed. Total resources and planned use of those funds are clearly described and determined and known. A unified budget eliminates an outgrowth of separate funds and separate financial goals, special group fund-raising campaigns, competing organizations, and a multiplicity of bank accounts and extra, unnecessary bank service charges.

A unified budget, by retaining all of the congregation's resources in one account and on one financial statement, shows the total activity and stewardship of the congregation. It presents a total view of all the activities of the congregation in contrast to the often partial statement of resource use and allocation represented by separate church budgets. Unfortunately, the trend among congregational groups is away from such a budget because it is not understood and donors are often eager to have more control over the use of their gifts. While that complicates the financial record-keeping and reporting process, it probably does accentuate for some people specific programs and needs and may indeed increase giving.

A capital budget, distinct from the operating budgets of the church, is yet another kind of church budget. A capital budget specifies sources and uses of funds for a certain building project or major repair project. It will carefully describe how the project will be financed. And it is a very appropriate scriptural kind of budget: "For which of you, desiring to build a tower, does not first sit down and count the cost, whether he has enough to complete it?" (Luke 14:28 RSV).

Capital budgets are usually line-item budgets because they list, item by item, how the funds are going to be spent for land, construction, landscaping, fees, furniture, interest, and other costs. Proper accounting procedures are used to release these funds under controlled appropriation and to prevent overspending and multiple authorizations, and to provide assurance to the congregation of careful trusteeship of funds.

Budgets for major capital projects are kept separate from benevolences or current operating budgets of the congregation. And when inflation is soaring a frequent updating of budget estimates will be required if cost overruns are to be avoided. A capital spending budget is maintained as long as the project is under construction.

A debt retirement budget, on the other hand, is also a handy management tool in new building control for congregations caught in the inflation squeeze. This kind of budget specifies the way in which the congregation expects to meet its debt commitments on a building or on some other major project. Such budgets are created for the life of the loans involved in the project. Special fund-raising programs may generate the intitial funds for the project. Later transfers might be made from current operating budgets or other budgets to supplement additional commitments. Generally, the debt retirement budget is developed once the capital project budget is completed. Such budgets help the congregation not only to control spending but also to maximize earnings before the funds are actually needed for building or debt retirement.

Thus, church budgets do come in all kinds of shapes and sizes. Certainly there is not just one kind of budget, and congregational leaders should be aware of the need to prepare separate budgets for different needs.

One response to inflation is to break out some of the cost centers from the usual church budget, centers that are not operating budget items necessarily, and report on these separately. A much clearer picture of the congregation's financial status can be obtained that way.

For example, one congregation reports separately on a variety of special funds and activities with individual reports made on the use of all memorial funds, on the building fund, on the use of benevolence dollars. Separate reports also show how much the congregation spends to make its facilities available to community groups such as the election board, a dance group, Alcoholics Anonymous, wedding receptions for nonmembers, highway department hearings, and a birth control clinic. Yet another report lists all the new equipment purchased, renovations, and building use changes. One report analyzes utility costs month by month before zoning changes were made and after a reassignment of class use to utilize the zone changes more fully. Yet another report shows the costs of maintaining the parsonage and lists all improvements.

Your lay leaders will certainly decide how the reporting is to be done. But one thing is certain: the CPI does make a difference in the congregation's budget-making process. Costs for operating a church program go up the same as anyone's costs go up, differently perhaps, but nevertheless up.

Whatever creative response to inflation the congregation embarks on next, it will no doubt always be reflected in a budget.

Borrow Money Now or Wait?

Inflation has certainly had an impact on the way in which new or renovated church buildings are financed. When inflation-induced high interest rates (or was it vice versa?) impact on church construction (on all contruction, for that matter) the result can be disastrous. When interest rates are high, church building virtually comes to a standstill for those congregations that expected to borrow money to build.

It is simply too expensive to borrow. Even a church bond program in which bonds are sold to members—sometimes a successful way to raise borrowed money—can turn out to be expensive (high interest to stimulate sales) and difficult (unattainable goals, inability to repay, missed interest, etc.).

Congregations, therefore, generally must go about financing the construction of new buildings in new and different and creative ways. According to Ashley Hale, borrowing for whatever reason and by whatever procedure to build is best avoided, not necessarily because of high interest, but because there's just more money available by asking before you build.

He writes in *The Clergy Journal* that the church mortgage is as traditional as apple pie, baseball, and the 4th of July.

> But today at least 75 percent of all church mortgages are unnecessary. Fund-raising techniques have improved.
>
> True, very young churches often, but not always, must build new facilities that they cannot yet pay for. True, churches relocating that cannot sell their old property advantageously often, but not always, must move into new buildings before they are paid for. But most mortgages are incurred by neither new nor relocating churches; they are incurred by churches that could raise the money instead of borrowing it.
>
> Yet, many a church has paid, in principal and interest, for a new building twice—or even three times—over. Paying for a new building out of the budget is the slowest and most expensive way a church can go.

The amount of money that a congregation will give to a building fund campaign is almost always underestimated. But the record is clear: in competently-managed campaigns for maximum goals, 85% of American and Canadian churches can raise as much for a building fund in three years as the members will give to the annual operating budget for the same period. About 15% of the churches can raise twice that much.

The church saddled with a mortgage that tries to make significant, vigorous forward movement is likely to experience the ultimate in congregational frustration. It's like running the 220 high hurdles carrying an 80-pound knapsack. The conservative members of the Board—and even of the congregation—will always vote against a proposal for a new venture that involves increased expenditures ". . . until we pay off the mortgage," even though the mortgage may be for 20 or 30 years.

Adding a big debt-service item to the budget seldom generates a commensurate increase in the members' giving. Paying for debt retirement is a cheerless sort of thing. It has no "power to stir men's souls." (Or women's either, for that matter.) We have a term for what happens because a capital-fund item crowds its way into an operations budget: "program deficits." Something has to give, and debt-payments can't.

Mr. Hale's solution is that gifts from the capital of individual members should be secured more aggressively than is now done by most congregational building-fund-raising programs. Modest gifts to current budgets can turn into magnificent gifts for a building fund if potential donors are asked. The result will be a spiritual impact upon good giving and great living in that congregation. Furthermore, operating-budget giving often jumps at the end of the building fund pledge payment period, but not always. But Mr. Hale's final advice in this article was clearly: "Raise all that you can and only then think about borrowing."

In today's economy it is important to maximize

resources that have been secured for a building until they must be paid out for construction. This requires careful and prudent investing of the funds. In a year's time, for example, due to increases in interest income received, the available funds for a project can go up by 10 to 12 percent. As inflation ebbs—if and when it does—that increase will significantly add to the dollars available for construction, especially if the cost of money stays high even though inflation rates go down, as was the case in mid-1982. Typically, though, interest rates should fall whenever inflation rates fall. If they do, the impact of careful financing will still be to maintain the same value of those dollars given.

People have the money to give, but they must be asked, says Mr. Hale. And when asked, payment should be sought as soon as possible, quickly invested, and prudently protected until as much as possible has been received. Then construction can begin. Perhaps something will need to be borrowed, maybe, but best not.

V

A Potpourri of
Creative Responses
to Inflation

Creative responses to handling inflation in a congregation are limited only by the imagination of the lay and professional staff leaders of that group. In this book I have explained many such responses and know that each reader could suggest many more.

More than anyone else, perhaps, Lyle Schaller, editor of this series of books, has set forth succinctly yet other important alternative ways in which congregational leaders can respond to inflation. Here's his listing from the April 1981 issue of *The Parish Paper:*

Here are sixteen responses that various congregations have used in seeking to offset the impact of inflation.

1. One of the most widely used courses of action has been to reduce the payroll. Sometimes . . . this has been accomplished by replacing a full-time employee with a part-time staff person.

More often it has meant salary increases of five or six or seven percent per year, which is substantially less than the increases in wages and salaries for the general population or the increase in Social Security payments or the increase in the Consumer Price Index.

Other churches have gone from paid to volunteer staff persons for youth ministries, music, secretarial and office work, custodial help or visitation.

Scores of middle-sized congregations have followed a similar policy by changing from a full-time resident minister to a part-time pastor. In some cases the minister serves two or more congregations, but there has been a sharp increase in the number of ministers serving one church on a part-time basis while holding a secular job.

Another approach to reducing payroll costs in many larger churches has been to replace a full-time ordained associate minister with lay staff.

While this response to inflation can be defended in some overstaffed congregations and in those churches that have resigned themselves to the inevitability of numerical decline, reducing the payroll may be counterproductive in growing churches and in those with the potential for growth.

2. A more attractive alternative is to cut expenditures by reducing energy costs. One congregation in Maine, for example, reduced its fuel oil consumption by one-half in one year through a series of energy conservation measures. These were paid for by a special financial appeal outside the regular budget.

3. A similar approach has been followed by several congregations that have responded to the fact that frequently it is easier to raise money for capital expenditures than for operating needs. These churches take all capital expenditures out of the regular budget and finance these by designated second mile gifts. This frees the operating budget, which is supported by the regular weekly contributions, for the increases necessary to offset the fact that consumer prices increased by 88% between December 1973 and December 1980.

4. An even more productive, but also more complex system has been followed by an increasing number of congregations that prepare three budgets—one for basic operating expenditures, a second for capital costs including major maintenance items and a third for missions. The operating budget is financed by the weekly offerings and regular pledges while the other two budgets are supported by designated contributions via special offerings.

5. Another approach, also based on the preference by an increasing number of lay persons for designated giving and the decreasing support for the unified budget, is the "second chance appeal." Since God gives each of us a second chance, this procedure offers church members a second chance to offset the impact of inflation. If pledges for the upcoming year

are sought in the autumn, during the following March or April members are given a choice of two or three special projects for designated "second mile" giving. Some congregations offer a "third chance" the following September or October. In practice, if this is done each year, and if the special projects represent believable needs, it results in special gifts equivalent to 10 or 15 percent of the total budget. If it is done twice a year, it usually results in total extra giving equal to 15 to 20 percent of the total budget.

One system for implementing this is to ask the members to respond to one or more of three or four special needs that are presented in a once-a-year appeal. A common package includes a special appeal for extra financial support for (1) a special mission cause, (2) a local program need such as expansion of the music program, (3) a capital need such as purchase of a van or replacement of the heating plant or an energy conservation system and/or (4) support for a new community outreach ministry. Members can choose from among these needs and designate their special gift.

6. In a growing number of the very large congregations—the 8% of all churches that include one-third of all Protestant church members on the North American continent—a shift to electronic data processing for financial and membership records has provided more information for the members and reduced the costs of record keeping.

7. One of the most widespread responses to inflation has been to deter certain expenditures until a future day.

The most obvious of these has been to defer to a later date building maintenance.

The most subtle has been to defer program expenditures and the expansion of the program in response to new needs.

Perhaps the most serious has been to defer to a later date expenditures for new programs and ministries for children, youth, and young adults—and thus miss a whole generation of future church members.

In some denominations the decision was made to defer to a future generation the current costs of pension for ministers. In the United Methodist Church, for example, the unfunded liability for ministerial pensions has nearly doubled since 1967 and is approaching $600 million.

Eventually deferred costs come due in one form or another.

8. While it seldom is mentioned, one of the most

widespread responses to inflation has been to encourage the minister's wife to seek employment outside the home.

Today approximately three out of five women married to a pastor are employed outside the home, double the proportion of 1955.

9. While it is only beginning to be the pattern in the mainline denominational churches, one of the most productive, and also one of the most theological and biblically defensible responses represents a major change in church finances. Over the years many congregations drifted into the practice of asking members to make a financial commitment or pledge to a church budget. This is in sharp contrast to asking members to tithe their income.

One of the implications of the change is in the psychological response produced by rapid inflation. When a member learns the church budget has doubled in eight years, the natural response may be, "Why? That's too much of an increase in only eight years when our membership total has remained on a plateau!"

A different response is elicited when the church member is asked to reflect on the fact that his or her income has doubled in eight years and, on the average, tripled in only fourteen years.

In other words, one of the most effective responses to inflation is to stress Christian stewardship rather than underwriting a church budget!

10. One of the operational expressions of Christian stewardship that is gaining support sometimes is referred to as Grace Giving. The basic assumption is that it is only through the grace of God that we live to see another day and that all our material possessions are given to us by the grace of God.

The operational application of this concept has three dimensions to it. First, the financial commitment of a member is between that individual and God, not between the member and the congregation. When financial pledges are made, each person or family signs a pledge card indicating the amount of money they intend to contribute to that congregation during the coming year. That pledge card is placed in an envelope with the member's name on the outside. The envelope is sealed and turned in with the other pledges, perhaps in a special ceremony on a particular Sunday. It is never opened! At the end of the year, the unopened envelope is returned to the member with a statement of how much money that member gave during the year.

The second operational component is that the finance committee prepares a budget on the basis of needs rather than on anticipated income. After all, if we live by the grace of God and if it is God who gives us another day, is it not reasonable to assume that God will provide for our needs, both individually and corporately?

Third, since a congregation lives by the grace of God, it is not necessary to lay aside reserves for the future. The congregation promises to spend or give away all the money received during the year. Insofar as is administratively possible, the congregation will end up the year with a zero balance.

11. A less radical approach is the Faith-Promise system. Basically this means asking each member to make a financial commitment for the coming year based on their expectation of their income. In an inflationary era sinful people tried to underestimate their anticipated income. Therefore, the faith pledge is accompanied by the promise that if the member's actual income exceeds expectations, that member promises to give the church a tithe of the additional income.

12. One of the most remarkable responses to the pressures of inflation appears to be based on the promise that while many people have a rather pessimistic view of the future for the world in general, most of them have a lot more money than they ever had before. The increase in the number of persons eating meals away from home is evidence of the second half of this premise.

The operational application of this concept is to raise a large amount of money in cash in one day. Dozens of churches have found that if the cause is attractive and if that special day is preceded by an adequate informational effort, it is possible to raise in one special offering an amount equal to between one-third of the annual budget and twice the annual budget. A few churches have raised in one day an amount equal to three times the annual budget! The most common appeals are either (a) missions or (b) building programs.

13. A few congregations have responded to the bias in the tax laws by (a) asking members to pay in advance a two-year financial commitment, thus enabling the church to draw a high rate of interest on a large cash balance, (b) encouraging the members to borrow money to do this, thus gaining a big

income deduction for that one year and taking the standard deduction for the second year, and (c) giving the members an income deduction on the interest paid while the church does not have to pay taxes on the interest it receives.

14. More and more churches are encouraging members to make their contribution in the form of stocks and other assets that have appreciated in value, rather than in cash, thus giving the member a tax advantage.

15. While the number is still small, many congregations with very large buildings to maintain are encouraging members to remember the church in their wills and are financing the maintenance and repairs of the building from bequests and legacies.

16. One of the least painful, but most effective responses is better reporting. In many churches a financial squeeze may be a symptom of the basic problem of inadequate communication. The use of visual communication, such as slides, motion pictures, posters, and dramatic presentations, can help improve the quality of communication and enable the members to understand the financial needs of that congregation.

Which of these responses will help your church live with inflation?

The Story of a Miracle

A perfect example of Lyle Schaller's twelfth suggestion above is the story of the miracle of gifts in one day for the High Street United Methodist Church in Muncie, Indiana. When fire and explosion raced through the church building one winter day in 1980, the result was an explosion of gifts that raised $1,120,000 in a single day! A carefully orchestrated publicity program, along with the influence of church and community leaders and the sacrificial giving of many members, helped to cap off the congregation's most successful fund-raising program ever. According to the leaders of the congregation, careful planning, some sizable advance gifts, and the inspiration of some who had done it before in other places helped to raise the sights of the people to what could be done.

Not waiting for an inspiration on how to raise the money to restore (above the $2.1 million available from insurance), the congregation began rebuilding on faith. Then the leaders listened carefully to every possible suggestion on raising the rest of the money needed to meet the estimated $4 million reconstruction cost.

After listening to someone who had "done it before" in another congregation, the leaders met and made their commitment "to go for cash." At a congregational meeting the program was carefully and thoroughly explained. Five hundred members listened and then went home and got to work. On a Sunday morning in December, two and a half months away, the cash gifts would be placed on the altar of the yet unfinished sanctuary.

The spirit and closeness of the congregation was thrilling to watch, reported the pastor. While some larger gifts were committed to motivate, the less wealthy members raised cash in many ways. One member sold a leather coat, a woman sold her platinum wristwatch, a middle-class family with small children took out a bank loan for $2,500. And when that December Sunday arrived even all of Muncie, not just the members of the congregation, were excited.

This was not a monument, said the pastor, "this was a wilderness experience in futility, trauma, trouble and pain with positive results." This was a building, to be sure, but a building for the sake of building is not the church; the church building is only the "identifiable base" for the program and mission of the congregation. This was "an outward expression of an inner faith."

When the offertory came that day, 1,200 members and friends filed by the altar and in 35 minutes had left $1,120,000 of cash there. The new building was debt free!

Using the Consumer Price Index and Tax Law to Develop a Clergy Compensation Plan

Aside from the dramatic increases in the cost of utilities, there has probably not been a more significant increase in church budget costs than the compensation paid to the professional staff. Increases in the CPI have simply demanded comparable increases in staff salaries in order to be fair and to keep key persons employed. But the impact on the church budget has put total compensation costs at an increasingly higher proportion of the total budget. So, along with energy costs that continue to rise, salaries keep on going up, too.

Fortunately, there are ways in which the impact on the church budget may be lessened while at the same time retaining staff and providing to church professionals a total pay package that keeps up with inflation, at least reasonably well, without an equal increase in cost to the church. This is done by planning compensation commitments more thoroughly, considering tax laws and salary surveys of other professionals, and reviewing carefully how assigned responsibilities are fulfilled.

But because of special tax breaks to employees especially, lay leaders of congregations are in an unusual position to increase the take-home pay of their clergy and lay staff without necessarily increasing the cost to the church as much. Inflation's impact on staff compensation requires lay

68169

leaders to look much more carefully at the procedures used in planning compensation.

Clergy compensation planning hasn't always been done very well. There was a time, not so long ago, when a minister was paid $1,500 a year, given 40 acres to farm, a cow, and such fresh meat, eggs, and vegetables as generous church members might provide. Times have changed, of course, and ministers no longer need to farm and milk, as well as preach, in order to support their families and make ends meet.

Yet, a pastor's pay is still not what it ought to be. Many clergy salaries are still near the bottom end of the pay scale and often are increased in only the most cursory way. In fact, ministers are being taken advantage of and imposed upon in a way that congregations should not tolerate.

Far too many congregations have actually failed to take their responsibility seriously. In addition, too many pastors, fearful of antagonizing members or reluctant to express overt concern about money matters, have failed to confide in trusted members about the actual circumstances of their personal financial needs. As a result, congregations have assumed that the pastor's compensation was adequate, while pastors, frustrated in their desire to serve the congregation competently, have fretted about their inability to make ends meet. In the face of inflation's dramatic impact on costs, some clergy families are simply unable to cope.

Fortunately, many congregational leaders have taken significant steps to review their pastor's compensation quite carefully. They have become familiar with the unique income tax benefits applicable to clergy, many of which are effective only if the congregation takes certain specific advance action. They are aware of the steady and persistent rise in the cost of living and know their pastor is affected as much as they are by constant inflation in food, insurance, transportation, and medical and other costs.

More congregational leaders are also critically evaluating the effectiveness of their pastor's ministry, studying per-

101

formance, confidentially discussing personal financial worries, and discovering, perhaps for the first time, what the pastor's personal frustrations, ambitions, and goals really are.

Many denominations have taken specific steps to assist congregations in developing helpful procedures for establishing adequate salary levels for their pastors. Among the more extensive discussions have been the Guidelines for Clergy Compensation prepared by the Lutheran Church in America. Many congregations have effectively adapted these particular guidelines for their own use. They have learned that failure to meet the impact of inflation on clergy compensation could possibly lead to serious consequences in their relationships with their pastor.

Too Little Pay

Low pay due to inflation's persistent inroads into the value of the dollar can have serious consequences on the effectiveness of the pastor's ministry. Consider what can happen when pay is too low:

1. Low pay can interfere with the efficiency and productivity of your pastor's ministry to you and your congregation. Think about your own income. When you worry about how you can ever make ends meet, your job performance suffers. You fret that there won't be money to pay the dentist or piano teacher or the next life insurance premium. You worry about the rent or the mortgage payment. Your pastor worries, too, when pay is low. And that worry may be felt in the way sermons come across, or time spent in fewer hospital visits, or concern expressed for the special problems of others. Worry about money is bound to impinge upon your pastor's time for creative ministry. Don't let that happen. Prevent your pastor's preoccupation with finances by making sure your congregation pays enough and that you pay it right.

2. You can enhance the image of your pastor in the community with pay that is fair. Too often the people out

there perceive the pastor as low paid. They may even know that he or she is low paid. Of course, if you pay more, you can change that view. But until you do and until people know, most people will assume your pastor is not very well paid.

That's because pastors have traditionally been low paid (although the pattern has improved). It is an image that is hard to correct. So clergy still get discounts to the movies, free tickets to ball games, reduced prices on some airlines, and an abundance of gifts from members. My own pay at a church in the country a few years ago was always supplemented by fresh vegetables, eggs, milk, and meat from the gardens and homes of those members. And I was expected to make money somehow on the free use of the forty acres of pastureland that was part of the package, too! But the congregation knew I was low paid. The community knew it, too. These acts were their way of making that low pay seem larger. The image was there as well. And it will be at your church, too, unless you change the picture.

3. It is important for clergy to have a positive attitude toward the church they serve. It is important for you, too. But when inflation is high and pay is low, negative attitudes in either spouse in the parsonage family are more likely to be expressed. And that can't be good for the church. It's hard enough to minister effectively when one's outlook is positive and creative. But a negative attitude only makes the job more difficult. Avoid the negative, accentuate the positive. Consider the CPI as well. Pay your pastor enough.

4. As long as inflation spirals upward at unheard of rates (although it's getting better), your pay and your pastor's pay are going to be seriously affected. It's hard enough to keep up with climbing grocery bills, much more so to pay orthodontists, school fees, summer camp, and flute teachers. When pay is restricted to something less than preferable, the burden is almost overwhelming. Has the salary you pay to your pastor kept up with his or her expenses? Inflation is

disastrous. But it's impossible when your pastor's spendable income is less and less even though you pay more and more.

5. Moonlighting is a temptation for any minister when income won't match outgo. And clergy have a unique opportunity to earn a second paycheck. After all, the ministry is not an eight-to-five job. Usually—beyond the required Sunday mornings and perhaps Wednesday evenings—the job is whenever the pastor wants to put in the time. When income is low and the chance to earn a few extra dollars comes along, many clergy will jump at the opportunity. It's a way to help pay the grocer and the doctor and those fast-food places, too. Moonlighting is one way people cope with inflation.

But moonlighting, doing another job, always interferes with ministry. A pastor's time cannot be scheduled so precisely. Emergencies do come up. People do need to be visited. Committee meetings happen all the time. And there's always someone needing to talk with the pastor. Ministry will be hurt when a second job is needed.

Avoid the possibilities. Keep your pastor on the job and available for the job, full time. Pay enough.

6. The spouses of many clergy (more than half, probably) work outside the home, often of necessity. When inflation persists and pay doesn't match, many spouses do bring home that second paycheck simply because the first one is not enough. If you'd like to see more of your pastor's spouse around the church, maybe you should look into why that spouse works. It may be money, although it could be for self-fulfillment or satisfaction or many other reasons. But when it's for money, as it most often is, the congregation loses out on what could have been a useful pair of workers. You've called a minister, not the spouse, but often that ministry is enhanced by an involved spouse. It may be your choice, depending on what you pay.

7. Low-paid pastors often end up with low pensions, too. Depending on your denomination's pension plan, the higher

paid pastors may get more pension because more money keeps going into the fund for them than for others. When a percentage of current salary is the basis for pension plan contributions, the better paid are better pensioned. Low pay may make a difference in your pastor's pension. Better check it out to see the real difference it makes. It could be significant.

8. There is a limit, and some clergy simply drop out of the ministry because they can no longer afford it. There's more pay in something else. And if they believe they need more than you pay and can find it someplace else, many go. They may enjoy the ministry, they will miss the ministry, probably; but the reality of what you pay determines the choice. Some other position pays more. Low pay can provoke that change.

9. Perceived low pay will not bring more young people to ministry. It will only turn them away. To attract and keep the brightest and most promising men and women means pay has got to be attractive and stay that way. Not only that, but young adults need to know that pay will be commensurate with responsibility and ability. If it is, the profession attracts the best; if it isn't, some of the best will go someplace else. What you pay your pastor has a profound affect on how a prospective student will view the nature of the ministry.

No pastor expects to be wealthy. Yet, for you, me, or anyone else, adequate income is necessary for the fulfillment of the responsibilities and obligations you know you should honor. When inflation soars, it simply means more cost for congregations for professional staff.

Compensation

Sometime during the year a congregation puts together its annual budget. By whatever means it puts that new program together, it is particularly critical that serious consideration be given to changes in the pastor's compensation. See that it

105

is. With costs always going up, adequate salary increases are imperative for your pastor if you expect your pastor's ministry to remain effective.

It is important to lift the sights of your members to the point where they recognize the pastor's service in an appropriate way, monetarily. Salary, of course, becomes the base of any compensation plan. Then there's a housing allowance (or parsonage), pension plan arrangement, Social Security allowance, health insurance premiums, vacation time, sick leave benefits, continuing education possibilities, a car allowance, professional expense reimbursements, and a whole host of other matters.

Since the pastor's pay package is made up of all those items, and perhaps others, it's important that you carefully consider all the factors that influence each item. For example, you'll want to be familiar with the income tax rules that affect that pay and allowance; with the current rate of increase in the CPI; with the Social Security tax on clergy income; and with ways in which adequate professional expense reimbursements, vacation time, continuing education op- portunities, and many other types of compensation can be made available at a reasonable cost to the congregation.

Since the minister's pay package often includes many items that are not real income, yet are a cost to the congregation, it's important to separate real earnings from other payments that are merely reimbursements of profes- sional expenses. Your pastor's real income is what has been earned, the wages your congregation has paid. Other payments may include reimbursement of professional expenses, such as a car allowance. But that is not compensation, even though it is part of the congregation's cost for having a pastor and doing business.

For most clergy, total compensation is often incorrectly calculated to include both earnings and reimbursements for professional expenses. It's important, therefore, that you make the distinction between the two clear to your official board. After all, the congregation's total costs for having a minister, that is, the amount included in the budget for all of the expenses associated with paying for a pastor, are not all necessarily income to the pastor. It's not all take-home pay. True, the cost is the same to the congregation either way. But for the pastor, it is important that the congregation be aware of salary separate and apart from its total cost of paying for a pastor. Unless your congregation is aware of the true income they pay your pastor, they may assume it's a great deal more than it really is. Consequently, the pastor will only come out on the short end.

An effective way of clarifying this kind of distinction and thus visualizing more dramatically the impact of inflation on the costs for having a pastor is to list the congregation's expenses for having a pastor in more than one budget classification. After all, your congregation doesn't list postage under salaries, and benevolences are not a part of office expenses. Neither should car allowances, for example, which are transportation or travel costs, or mortage payments on the parsonage, which is debt reduction, be part of salary. These are unrelated to compensation, and should not be shown in the same category of expenses as the pastor's salary.

Thus, only base salary and housing allowance should be included in the professional salaries category of the congregational budget. The congregation's payment of pension contributions, health insurance premiums, and other supplemental benefits should be listed as part of professional fringe benefit costs, along with the costs for providing similar benefits to other employees. Separating out specific costs also helps identify those items most affected by inflation and thus perhaps needing closer evaluation.

Reimbursements to your pastor for professional expenses should be included among the congregation's operating budget-line expense items. Thus a car allowance is in fact part of the congregation's travel costs. Postage or supplies you buy are part of the congregation's administrative expenses. Payments on the parsonage mortgage are debt-retirement costs. The distinctions and cost increases of each are important.

Your pastor's real pay, therefore, includes only such items as base salary, housing allowance, utility allowance, the congregation's contribution to a pension plan, health insurance allowances (or the premiums paid by the congregation), Social Security allowances, and such similar items which are strictly compensation, real and effective income to your pastor.

The Plan

Lay leaders have elected all kinds of procedures for reviewing compensation with their pastors. Some merely let the banker or stockbroker in the church set the pay. Others at least ask a committee of two or three leading citizens to recommend an amount. Some let the congregation debate the issue in full view of the pastor and spouse. Most start with salary and let the other pieces, if any, just fall into place. The concerned congregational leader, however, selects the committee and then leaves the pay plan up to the committee or the official board. Intelligent consideration of pay plans includes a full review of all the issues by a selected group of dedicated leaders.

A recommended approach for going over your pastor's pay is to consider first reimbursement, then supplemental benefits, and finally housing and salary.

Reimbursements

1. *Professional costs.* Your goal is full reimbursement of those costs incurred by your pastor professionally. These are costs for the benefit of your congregation, such as costs for transportation (car expenses), church supplies, gifts to

108

members, books, subscriptions to professional journals, continuing education, dues, and such, all of which are affected by inflation.

Keep in mind that reimbursements are precisely that—reimbursements, not compensation, as has previously been emphasized. These are congregational costs for having a pastor. They will show up on your budget as expense items, perhaps large expenses, but reimbursements are not compensation. Be sure your committee has a clear concept of that understanding. Reimbursements are paid to the pastor, and they are a cost to your congregation. They are not income to the pastor.

With the Internal Revenue Service now insisting that most clergy are employees for income tax purposes (clergy are still self-employed for Social Security tax purposes), it has become all the more important for your congregation to have an adequate reimbursement plan. A good plan is a way to help your pastor save some tax dollars.

Those unreimbursed professional expenses that you may have forced your pastor to pay in the past may no longer be deductible on the pastor's income tax return if your pastor is an employee and does not itemize deductions. You can do your pastor a big favor and cut his or her income tax by making sure you reimburse in full for all professional expenses. It's a reasonable personnel policy, and it just may be a way to boost your pastor's net take-home pay. (Clergy list car expenses now on Form 2106, other unreimbursed expenses on Schedule A of Form 1040).

2. *Car expenses.* The cost for using a personal automobile on church business is probably by far the largest of all of your pastor's professional expenses. If you've adopted the policy that you are going to reimburse the pastor for all those costs, then you must decide how that will be done.

The ideal arrangement for making sure that you fully reimburse your pastor for the professional expenses he or she incurs for driving an automobile on church business is for

109

your congregation to provide the pastor with the exclusive use of a church-owned or -leased automobile. That way, the church, not the pastor, really assumes all the costs, as it should.

The least desirable way for your congregation to pay for those expenses is to make an annual payment or a monthly fixed payment to cover potential expenses. Usually that lump-sum payment has no relationship to the expenses that your pastor actually incurs. More often than not it was set some years ago and now, as the cost of everything continues to go up, is woefully inadequate. Your pastor probably has to dip down into salary to pay for car costs now. That shouldn't be. Don't let it happen. Salary is for personal expenses, not for the church's expenses!

A more ideal arrangement is for your congregation to pay a cents-per-mile reimbursement. Have your pastor estimate what it costs to operate his or her car per mile on church business, including replacement, and then pay that as an allowance. The pastor tells the treasurer each month how many miles have been driven on church business, and the reimbursement is promptly made.

It probably costs your pastor 25¢ or more a mile to operate an automobile. If so, that's what you ought to pay. IRS may allow only 20¢ a mile automatic deduction (1982 rate), but that's no assurance that that is the cost of operating a car. If you don't like the rate your pastor quotes, your congregation can always go out and lease or buy a car for the pastor to use. When the church pays actual costs you will know what it costs to operate a car—and it's more every year, another constant but necessary drain on the church budget.

You should know that for tax purposes it really makes no difference how much allowance you pay. A tax principle is not applicable here; a reimbursement principle is. For tax purposes IRS permits a deduction of 20¢ a mile for the first 15,000 miles and 11¢ for all additional miles (1982 rates), except that once 60,000 miles have been used at the 20¢ rate, all future miles are only 11¢ a mile.

Any car allowance you pay your pastor is taxable income. But expenses may be deducted, either at the automatic mileage rate noted above (for the current year) or actual expenses. Ministers who are employees will show those deductions on Form 2106. Self-employed persons would list the deductions on Schedule C of Form 1040.

When you are figuring total pay, don't add the car allowance to salary. It's not compensation. It's reimbursement of expenses and should not be added into the pastor's income. Of course, it is certainly a cost for having a pastor, but don't confuse it with salary.

Supplemental Benefits

1. *Pension plan contributions.* Retirement comes all too quickly for all of us. It does for your pastor, too. Thus, it is important that you be certain your congregation has made adequate plans to fund your pastor's retirement.

Most denominations have a pension plan program for their clergy. Many of these are self-funded plans by the church pension board; others are handled through an insurance company. Be certain that in whatever plan you are participating, applicable tax benefits are available to your pastor.

You should know that self-employment Keogh-type plans are not available to ministers on salary paid by the congregation. So says the IRS. Even though ministers may pay the self-employment Social Security tax, that does not make them self-employed for Keogh plan purposes. However, ministers are eligible now to participate in an Individual Retirement Account (IRA), even though they may also be participating in their employer's pension plan.

Tax-deferred annuities offer clergy another opportunity to accumulate pension dollars while deferring income tax on the

111

contribution and on the interest the fund earns. Such plans are a good supplement to any required pension plan and offer a good tax benefit and inflation hedge to clergy who pay income taxes anyway. Such contributions and interest earnings are taxable to your pastor only when finally received in retirement.

Be certain you understand your denomination's pension plan and how you can make contributions for the maximum tax benefit of your pastor. It's your responsibility as a key lay leader to be informed and to know how that matter is best handled. Your pastor should also know.

2. *Health, disability, and life insurance.* There is no excuse for your pastor's family to be without health insurance, including a major medical plan and disability benefits. A group term life insurance policy should also be part of that package, since many clergy may not have any or much life insurance on their own.

The cost of being sick is so high few ministers would be able to meet the cost personally if one of the family were hospitalized for even a short time, much less a longer stay. Since sickness is an event that is almost always unexpected, you should be certain there is coverage. It's a protection for your church, too, since a financially destitute pastor might become a financial burden on your congregation.

Premiums for health coverage (an ever-increasing cost!) should be paid by the congregation. There's an income tax benefit that way since health insurance premiums paid by an employer are not taxable income. Of course, all taxpayers who itemize their deductions on Schedule A are permitted to deduct medical expenses, including personally paid health insurance premiums, to the extent that such medical costs exceed 5% of adjusted gross income. But your pastor may not have enough unreimbursed medical expenses to deduct anything. Then payment of the health insurance premium

112

by the congregation means a full "deduction" of that amount. Of course, premiums paid by the congregation do not appear anywhere on your pastor's tax return. They are not additional income. Paying the premium is a way to increase the pastor's take-home pay (by reducing his or her taxes) yet not cost the congregation anything more.

While Social Security does provide disability coverage, it will probably not be adequate; thus it may be supplemented by the minister's own coverage. At any rate, that is a responsibility of your congregation, and the church should pay the premium. A disabled pastor could become a financial burden to a caring congregation if family financial resources are inadequate.

Group term life insurance premiums paid by the congregation are not taxable income to the minister up to $50,000 coverage. Any other life insurance premium paid by the congregation on a policy controlled by the pastor is taxable income. So your congregation can provide a tax benefit, while at the same time guaranteeing some insurance protection for your pastor's family, by participating in a group term life insurance plan. The congregation pays the premium.

3. *Social Security allowance.* Your pastor pays taxes, both income and Social Security taxes. Some lay leaders don't know that. Many members of congregations often believe that somehow their pastor is exempt from taxes. Not so. In fact, your pastor will pay 30% more Social Security tax in 1984 than you as an employee will pay and get nothing more for it. That's because clergy are required to pay the Social Security tax at the self-employment tax rate, while your congregation, as employer, pays nothing. (Beginning in 1984 all congregations are required to pay Social Security taxes on the wages of all employees, except the minister.)

Each year, as you know, the cost of Social Security goes up. In 1982 clergy paid a tax rate of 9.35%, up from 9.3% in 1981 and 8.1% in 1980. In 1983 the rate stays at 9.35%, but, as usual, the wage base goes up anyway to $35,700. In 1982 that base was $32,400, up from $29,700 in 1981 and $25,900 in 1980.

The new 1983 Social Security Act provides for increasing Social Security tax rates for employees and self-employed with a tax credit to help offset some of the increase. Tax rates for the next several years are as follows:

SOCIAL SECURITY TAX RATES

Year	Employee		Self Employed			
	Old Rate	New Rate	Old Rate	New Rate	Tax Credit	Effective Rate
1984	6.7%	6.7%	9.35%	14.00%	2.7%	11.3%
1985	7.05	7.05	9.90	14.10	2.3	11.80
1986	7.15	7.15	10.00	14.30	2.0	12.30
1987	7.15	7.15	10.00	14.30	2.0	13.02
1988	7.15	7.51	10.00	15.02	2.0	13.02
1989	7.15	7.51	10.00	15.02	2.0	13.02
1990	7.65	7.65	10.75	15.30	-0-	**

**The 1990 rate will be calculated on a different basis: the net income from self-employment is reduced by the employee tax that would be payable thereon (7.65% in 1990), and then the combined employer-employee tax rate (15.30% in 1990) is applied thereto, and finally, half of the taxes is deducted from the net income from self-employment in computing income tax liabilities.

Thus, for clergy earning the maximum wage base, the 1982 Social Security tax maximum was $3,029.40; the 1983 maximum $3,337.95. The maximum wage base each year is increased at the rate of increase in average wages during the previous year.

That, then becomes a significant tax burden for your pastor. Since congregations cannot pay the pastor's Social Security tax, that constantly increasing inflationary cost must come out of the pastor's paycheck, thus always reducing net take-home pay.

Nevertheless, no matter what the expense involved, clergy who remain in Social Security have tremendous potential benefits, as does anyone covered by Social Security. Not only is retirement income a possibility, but disability, survivor's, and Medicare insurance are part of Social Security, too, plus a death benefit in certain instances. And that can be a significant dollar benefit. Still, as good as the benefits are, if the cost is excessive and cannot be afforded, it becomes oppressive.

Social Security legislation does permit clergy to opt out of Social Security under certain conditions. Newly ordained clergy have until April 15 following the second year in which they earn at least $400 from ministry to request lifetime exemption from the Social Security tax on income from ministry. However, the only valid procedure and reason for a minister to request and obtain such exemption is by signing a Form 4361 and confessing a conscientious objection to the receipt of public insurance proceeds, such as Social Security. Generally, unless the minister's denomination has taken a similar stance, the exemption may not be granted. Or, if granted, it might be revoked by IRS later with back taxes assessed, if it is determined that such conscientious objection is really not genuine and that some other reason may have prompted the request for exemption.

The exemption is not available simply because the minister doesn't like Social Security or it is too expensive or an insurance representative has convinced him or her that better coverage is available through private investments and insurance. Conscientious objection is the only valid reason that a minister can use to request an exemption from Social Security.

Concerned congregations have taken steps to help their pastors meet that cost of Social Security—a constantly increasing cost—by providing an allowance for the Social Security tax. That allowance, paid to the pastor, is used to pay the tax, or at least part of it. Of course, the congregation is not required to pay any of that cost, but it is certainly helpful when such an allowance is provided.

The amount of the allowance could be equal to the maximum Social Security self-employment tax, or to the difference between what the pastor and other employees pay; or the congregation might pay whatever they would pay as an employer were they required to do so. (Employer tax is 7% in 1984 even though employee net tax is 6.7%.) Shifting the cost to the congregation is fair and equitable since all other employers must pay Social Security taxes on the wages paid to their employees.

Your pastor will include that allowance as part of taxable income for both income and Social Security tax purposes. But any net allowance, even after taxes, will be a help in meeting that rising cost. There is no tax benefit to your pastor when you provide an allowance for Social Security taxes, but the additional income will boost pay.

4. *Vacation, holidays, and a day off.* You really can't expect your pastor to work seven days a week, fifty-two weeks a year. *You* don't. Your pastor also needs some days off; specify days so they will be taken. Many clergy are so conscientious about their ministry, see so much that is not being done and needs doing, that they have a hard time taking time off. You should be certain time is taken.

Insist on four weeks' vacation. The congregation won't fall apart during that time with capable lay leaders like yourself to help with worship and bulletins and cleaning and teaching.

Pastors should get holidays, too, perhaps not on *the* day, but some other day. And one day a week off should be specified in fairness to your pastor and to the pastor's family. A clear understanding should be spelled out. If you don't provide that time, your pastor will burn out and the work of the church really won't get done.

5. *Continuing education.* Your pastor needs to keep up with current trends in theology, counseling, evangelism, steward-ship. Provide him or her the opportunity to take advantage of

the many programs available, and you'll benefit the church and the pastor, too. Provide the time, pay two weeks a year plus a three-month sabbatical after six years, all plus an annual one-month vacation. Then be sure you pay the costs, too. Adequate time and money for helping the pastor maintain and improve skills in ministry are very important to the vitality of your church.

If your congregation is interested in what's possible with a sabbatical leave program, here's what one congregation has done:

1. Definition: pastoral sabbatical is a leave of absence for self-betterment to further service in God's kingdom.

2. Six years of service at this church will be required before a leave is considered.

3. Leave not to exceed one year.

4. Replacement arrangements to be negotiated between the pastor and the church council.

5. A minimum of one year between staff sabbaticals will be required.

6. Financial support by this congregation will be for base salary, housing allowance, pension payments, insurance premiums (none of the foregoing to be increased during such leave), tuition costs and fees, mileage allowance to and from location of study. Any stipends or scholarships awarded to the pastor to be deducted from this support package.

7. All continuing education time and money is available to be used as part of the leave.

8. Vacation and continuing education provisions may not be accrued during sabbatical.

9. This policy is to be administered by the church council.

10. Any other arrangements not covered by these policies shall be the responsibility of the church council.

6. *An equity allowance.* If your pastor must live in the church-owned parsonage, then you want to consider an

equity allowance. This is not a housing allowance. An equity allowance is, among other things, simply additional compensation set aside in a special fund available to the pastor to provide for housing. Usually the fund is expected to be used as a down payment. The annual payment to the fund is typically equal to the inflationary increase in value of the parsonage or a certain percentage applied against salary. There is no tax benefit with an equity allowance, only an opportunity for the congregation to share with the pastor some of the equity of the parsonage. It's another hedge against inflation for the pastor. It can be a big help to a pastor in eventually providing housing when a parsonage is no longer available.

7. *Other benefits.* You've probably thought of other benefits that you'd like to provide.

a. An employee scholarship fund for children of all full-time staff persons in the congregation is a possibility. Any plan should be carefully reviewed with an attorney to be certain it does not become taxable income when paid out.

b. Key-man life insurance is intended to protect the congregation against financial loss if the pastor should die in office. The policy beneficiary is the church and the church owns the policy. There are no tax consequences for the pastor in this kind of arrangement so long as the pastor has no control over the policy.

c. A discretionary fund may be useful for your pastor. Be certain, however, that it is kept that way and that you or other members don't pry into its use.

d. Malpractice insurance has become much more popular. Some larger denominations provide the coverage on a blanket basis for all clergy.

e. Vision care, dental insurance, legal assistance, financial counseling, automobile insurance, all at the expense of the employer, are offered to many employees. It's worth considering for the pastor.

f. A medical reimbursement plan offers an opportunity to

have the congregation pay for certain unreimbursed medical expenses up to agreed limits without such payments being considered income to the pastor. When all of the congregation's full-time employees are included, there could be a significant benefit. You may want to review the possibility with legal counsel. As a minimum, paying for the cost of your pastor's annual physical examination should be a congregational expense.

Housing

The costs for the housing arrangement you have with your pastor are probably (1) the greatest tax benefit available to your pastor's family, yet (2) one of the most inflationary parts of your church budget. Section 107 of the Internal Revenue Code provides that the fair rental value of a church-owned house may be excluded from taxable income. It also provides that a housing allowance paid to the pastor in lieu of the church-owned home is not subject to income tax to the extent used to provide a home.

Almost all pastors receive one of these benefits—parsonage or housing allowance. Periodically your congregation ought to review your present situation and determine if the long-standing current arrangement is really the best for the pastor and for the congregation.

You should know that your official board must note in its minutes a specific allowance designating this amount before such allowance is applicable as a tax advantage. The matter cannot be handled retroactively. And it must be designated in advance of the time when it is paid or housing expenditures made.

Be sure your congregation considers the maximum housing allowance available even though this may be more than cash salary. The relationship to salary is not important. It can be any ratio, but, says the IRS, the housing allowance cannot exceed the fair rental value of the home including furnishings, plus the cost of utilities.

A salary of $15,000 with housing allowance of $5,000 can be rearranged, say, to $8,000 salary and $12,000 housing allowance. If the amount is then actually spent, it is excludable from taxable income. For income tax purposes, your pastor does not report as taxable income the fair rental value of a home, only any unused allowance. (The actual housing allowance paid to a pastor is however considered for Social Security taxable income.)

Many reasons can be cited why either the parsonage or the housing allowance may be the most helpful to your pastor and to your congregation. (For a thorough discussion of the pros and cons and the regulations affecting parsonage/housing allowance, please review my booklet *Housing for Clergy*. For information write to Church Management, Inc., P.O. Box 1675, Austin, TX 78767.)

What your congregation does about housing can affect the future financial situation of your pastor. A housing allowance offers an opportunity to build up equity in a home (taking advantage of inflation) anticipating retirement housing needs. It also has significant income tax advantage. If the congregation provides a parsonage, it should be thinking of ways to help the pastor provide for housing when a parsonage is no longer available, such as when the pastor retires, becomes disabled, or dies. The parsonage may be fine now, but how will the church help the pastor find housing when there is, for the pastor, no longer any church-owned, rent-free parsonage?

Maybe you can't do anything about your housing situation right now. But it's a good time to ponder the effect of your housing arrangement upon the pastor's well-being and the church's responsibility to provide adequate remuneration.

Salary

Whatever cash salary you pay should be sufficient, adequate, and a fair indication of the worth of your pastor to your congregation. When salary is set, you may want to consider age and experience of your pastor as well as the size of your congregation. However, it may be better to consider your pastor's ability to relate to other people and how your pastor handles all the problem situations facing him or her every day.

Even the wages paid to other professional people offers a benchmark for what you might pay your pastor. Or the median salary received by all wage earners in your community is a good comparison. The median salary of the ministers in your denomination might be helpful also.

Pay Plans and the CPI

1. A typical pay plan

—Minimum salary for senior pastor (80% of senior pastor's salary to associate with same number of years of experience)

Table 6.1

Years of Service	Adult members			
	Up to 300	300-600	600-900	Over 900
Up to 5 years	$15,580	$16,785	$17,720	$18,650
6 to 10 years	18,650	19,580	20,515	21,450
11 to 15 years	21,450	22,380	23,310	24,250
Over 15 years	24,150	25,180	26,110	27,040

—Free use of a church-owned home or housing allowance equal to at least 40% of base salary.

—Car allowance equal to at least the government's mileage allowance.

—A minimum of 13% of the sum of salary, housing allowance, and any Social Security allowance to be paid by the congregation to a pension plan.

—An allowance for Social Security taxes equal to the maximum self-employment Social Security tax.

—A health and death benefit insurance plan with all premiums to be paid by the congregation.

121

—At least four weeks vacation.

—Two additional weeks for continuing education with tuition payments made by the congregation.

—A three months sabbatical each six years of service with the same congregation.

—And, full reimbursement for all professional expenses.

2. *Another pay plan*

Other pay plans may be more complicated. Here's one that sets pay on the basis of time in the ministry without regard to the size of the congregation. However, it gives no consideration for merit, greater responsibilities, or special skills. For those lay leaders interested in a more detailed calculation for pay, this offers a way to do it.

Beginning the first year in the ministry, basic salary is $260 a week, increased by $10 a week for each year in the ministry. Reimbursement for automobile expenses is set at 25¢ a mile, including the cost of replacement. A provision for Social Security tax allowance is set at 10% of salary and housing.

The pastor is provided with a parsonage and all utilities or a $5,000 housing allowance. Pension plan contributions are 12% of salary and housing. Health coverage is $700 a year. A book and study materials allowance is also recommended, for which $500 a year is anticipated.

For a congregation using that pattern, costs would be something like this. (Future inflation rates are not included since any guess would only be speculative.)

Table 6.2	First Year	Tenth Year	Twentieth Year
Base salary	$13,250	$18,720	$23,920
Car allowance	3,750	3,750	3,750
Social Security allow.	1,850	2,370	2,890
Pension plan	2,650	3,390	4,130
Health insurance	700	700	700
Book allowance	500	500	500
Housing allowance	5,000	5,000	5,000
Costs to congregation	$27,970	$34,430	$40,890

Obviously that would not all be income to the pastor. The pastor's net take-home pay is much less than the congregation's total cost for having a pastor. Here is what the real income, supplemental benefits and expense reimbursements in this situation would be like:

Table 6.3

Real Income	First Year	Tenth Year	Twentieth Year
Base salary	$13,520	$18,750	$23,920
Social Security allow.	1,850	2,370	2,890
Housing allowance	5,000	5,000	5,000
Net take-home pay	20,370	$26,090	$31,810
Fringe benefits			
Pension plan	$ 2,650	$ 3,390	$ 4,130
Health insurance	700	700	700
Book allowance	500	500	500
	$ 3,850	$ 4,590	$ 5,330
	First Year	*Tenth Year*	*Twentieth Year*
Reimbursements			
Car allowance	$ 3,750	$ 3,750	$ 3,750
Total cost to congregation	$27,970	$34,430	$40,890

3. Another unique pay plan

In yet another plan the pastor can be paid at a rate comparable to the median family income of the geographical area in which the congregation is located. The plan includes three steps: agreement on a pay range, adjustment to that range according to the complexity of assigned responsibilities, and development of a fair rate of remuneration based on job proficiency.

Step One: The minimum of the pay range should be the

median family income of those persons living within the geographical area served by the church, adjusted downward for favorable tax benefits uniquely available to pastors. Median salaries in the area must be adjusted for inflation depending upon the years for which they were applicable.

Because the pastor received the free use of a parsonage or a housing allowance and is able to exclude the value of either from taxable income, thus reducing tax liability, a downward adjustment of the median should be considered according to this plan. Allowing for further real estate tax savings for a minister in a parsonage, the median is reduced further. The maximum rate of the range should be 150% of the minimum so calculated.

Step Two: Assigning a factor of 1 to 10 for less to greater complexity, the pastor's job assignment should be evaluated. These elements might be rated in this way: newly formed congregation, size of congregation, level of education in the congregation, counseling problems in the congregation, degree of expected pastoral participation in the church program, difficulty of the mission field, proficiency of lay leadership, level of secretarial and staff help, aid received from other pastors in the area.

Out of a possible 100, the percentage points above 50 would increase the minimum-maximum range upwards. Less than 50 would lower the range.

Step Three: A fair rate of remuneration would finally depend upon the proficiency of the pastor on the job. Consider: education (liberal arts degree, seminary training, graduate work), experience (as a pastor), length of service with this congregation, abilities as shepherd, teacher, counselor, administrator, representative of Christ in the community.

Then, using these criteria, a fair rate of remuneration is set somewhere between those established ranges.

For example, assume the median salary for your geographical area as determined by the Bureau of Labor Statistics is $24,280.

If the fair rental value of the parsonage is $4,000 (or a housing allowance of that amount is used), tax liability in the 22% range is reduced by approximately $880 for federal taxes, perhaps $400 for state taxes in the 10% range. Property taxes (estimated at $1,200) are also avoided in a parsonage (or as part of excludable housing allowance).

The weighted estimated median family income for the year, therefore, might be reduced from $24,280 to $21,800 ($24,280 less the sum of $880, $400, and $1,200) which becomes the minimum pay range. The maximum would be 1.5 times as much, or $32,700.

If the complexity of the job is rated to be 55, then the pay range should be adjusted upward by 5% assuming a 50% complexity as normal. The pay range is now $22,890 ($21,800 times 1.05) to $34,335 ($32,700 times 1.05).

If a fair rate of remuneration is then based upon proficiency at the job, and that is assumed to be at a mid-point between the minimum and maximum adjusted range, a remuneration (cash salary and housing) would be tagged at $28,567 ($21,800 plus $34,355 divided by 2).

(The foregoing three-step pay plan has been adapted from "Salary Guide for Pastors," produced by the Presbytery of Great Rivers, IL, United Presbyterian Church in the USA, Harold Sedrel author.)

Finally

You'll probably always get better results from your pastor by offering a merit increase and saying thanks that way. But inflation often gets in the way. A 6% increase in pay next year may only keep up with inflation.

Of course, your congregation will have to decide what to pay. Pay enough and your pastor will stay; pay too little and there may be a change. Some conversation will help to keep the dialogue going and the understandings accurate.

Pay plans run the gamut, but the basics are still the same.

Consider reimbursements first, then benefits, then housing and salary. Understand the reason for each, establish the principle to be applicable, consider costs, and arrange the budget right. Mutual understanding will be critical to the development of a successful plan for next year.

What your congregation pays your pastor is your business, of course, but when you've considered the possibilities, examined the issues, understood the tax consequences, and know what is pay and what is simply a cost to the congregation and reimbursement to the pastor, you will be able to put a financial plan into shape that meets the inflationary impact of current CPI rate increases. It's not something you can do overnight. So, take your time. But begin your planning now for the next year. It's never too soon to plan!

At the End

Don't take my word for it, but I am convinced inflation will always be around. It always has been, although in greater or lesser degree from year to year. Yet, as inflation bounces around from less than 1% to more than 12% in various years, the challenge to managing congregational resources in that kind of complex economy will tax the ingenuity of even the most creative and dedicated church leaders.

This book has offered some pointers to better resource management, but the real key to the way in which your congregation's finances are managed will be you. How you give, how you lead, how you respond, how you tell others of your own stewardship response, how you help manage and plan the use of your congregation's resources, the way in which you are instrumental in developing meaningful, useful, and progressive compensation plans, the way in which you witness to the mission of the church—all this can be effective in the way in which your congregation's finances are managed in this constantly changing economy.

God always expects great things from his children. That expectation, I am convinced, is no less from you and the other congregational leaders in a time of severe testing of the use of existing financial resources. Solutions to every financial problem your congregation faces are possible. But you'll have to look for them, be creative in your thinking, and be willing to change strategy as the economy changes. You are indeed a steward and a giver and a manager and a planner. Your personal response and witness will often be the key to financing your congregation's programs in this complex and ever changing economy.

Bibliography

Espie, John C. *Handbook for Local Financial Record System*. Nashville: Abingdon Press, 1977.

Gray, Robert N. *Managing the Church: Business Methods and Church Business Administration*. vols. I and II. Austin: Church Management, Inc., 1971.

Gross, Malvern J., Jr. *Nonprofit Organizations, Financial and Accounting Guide*, 2nd ed. New York: Ronald Press, 1974.

Heyd, Thomas. *Planning for Stewardship: Developing a Giving Program for Congregations*. Minneapolis: Augsburg Publishing House, 1977.

Holck, Manfred, Jr. *Accounting Methods for the Small Church*. Minneapolis: Augsburg Publishing House, 1961.

———. *Annual Budgeting*. Minneapolis: Augsburg Publishing House, 1977.

———. *Cash Management*. Minneapolis: Augsburg Publishing House, 1978.

———. *Complete Handbook of Church Accounting*. Englewood Cliffs, N.J.: Prentice-Hall, 1978.

———. *Making It on a Pastor's Pay*. Nashville: Abingdon Press, 1974.

———. *Money and Your Church*. New Canaan, Conn.: Keats Publishing Co., 1974.

———. Editor & Publisher, *The Clergy Journal* magazine. Austin: Church Management, Inc., P. O. Box 1625, 78767. 10 times annually.

McCormally, Kevin, ed. *How to Get More for Your Money*. Washington, D.C.: The Kiplinger Washington Editors, Inc., 1981.

Poovey, W. A. *How to Talk to Christians About Money*. Minneapolis: Augsburg Publishing House, 1982.

Rieke Thomas C. and Espie, John C. *Opportunities in Stewardship*. Nashville: Discipleship Resources–Tidings, 1975.

Rudge, Peter F. *Management in the Church*. New York: McGraw-Hill, 1976.